Y0-BVQ-582

A Guide to Facilitating Cases
in Education

A Guide to Facilitating Cases in Education

Barbara Miller and Ilene Kantrov

HEINEMANN

Portsmouth, NH

Heinemann
A division of Reed Elsevier Inc.
361 Hanover St.
Portsmouth, NH 03801-3912
Offices and agents throughout the world

Library of Congress Cataloging-in-Publication Data
Barbara Miller
    A guide to facilitating cases in education/Barbara Miller and Ilene Kantrov.
      p.   cm.
    Includes bibliographic references .
    ISBN 0-435-07248-X
    1. Teachers—Training of. 2. Education—Study and teaching. 3. Case
method. 4. Social facilitation. I. Kantrov, Ilene. II. Title
II. Kantrov, Ilene.
  LB1707.M55 1998
    370'.71–dc21   97–27012
                                               CIP

Editor: Leigh Peake, Scott Mahler
Production: J. B. Tranchemontagne
Cover Design: Darci Mehall
Manufacturing: Louise Richardson

Printed in the United States of America on acid-free paper

01 00 99 98 97 DA 1 2 3 4 5 6 7 8 9

CONTENTS

PREFACE

While cases are appearing regularly in professional development programs, education course syllabi, and meeting agendas, there has not been as much discussion of what it means to facilitate cases. This book is designed to address that question. The premise on which this book is based is that case facilitation needs to be purposeful. That can seem like an obvious statement—Why wouldn't educators be purposeful in how they work with cases? However, many educators who use cases expect that the compelling ideas and creative solutions will be found within the case text itself. More often than not, the case text itself doesn't contain these essential elements. The compelling ideas and creative solutions need to come from the experience that is created around the case, from the discussion, reflection, and work that group participants do to learn from the case and from one another. This is where facilitation comes in, since it is a rare group that can manage this work on its own.

As a case facilitator, your role is to create a "case experience" through which the group can develop compelling ideas and creative solutions to the issues posed by the case. You can do this by how you structure the experience for participants and by how you interact with participants during discussion and other activities. One thing you can count on is that participants will bring a whole host of ideas and concerns to the case. Given that, you need to be actively involved in shaping the ensuing discussion. Don't be afraid to get involved. There is quite a bit of distance between shaping the discussion and dictating what people should think. Good facilitation means taking up the challenge of guiding the discussion, in light of what you know about the participants and their ideas, the case and its potential, and the goals for the case experience. This book describes how you can do that work in a thoughtful and purposeful way.

Facilitating cases in education is, for you, an opportunity for powerful growth and learning. You are not only providing a valuable service to a group as you assist it in its reflection about a case, but you are also opening yourself up to the chance to think about ideas in a new light, try different strategies, and increase your skills.

This book includes a lot of material about case facilitation and recommendations for things to do as you work with a group around a case. It is possible that you may feel overwhelmed in the face of all these ideas. You may wonder, "How can I possibly keep all these things in mind?" You can't—particularly if you are new at facilitation. That shouldn't stop you, though, from trying to facilitate a case and focusing on just a few of the ideas presented here. As you gain experience, you'll be able to attend to other issues. Your capacity to facilitate a productive discussion will increase as you incorporate more of the ideas in this book into your practice. Even if you disagree with what's said here or adapt it to your own situation or style, the act of considering how you want to act as a facilitator is important.

Case facilitation should be an opportunity for you to grow and learn as a professional. Set some goals for yourself in this work. Try a different strategy or consider a new idea about facilitation. Every group with which you work will present its own unique characteristics, and you can experience great variety just by working with different groups. However, don't rely on the differences among groups to be the only variety you have as a facilitator. Look beyond the group and decide how you want to expand your capacity as a facilitator to structure and guide engaging and productive discussions.

This book grows out of the authors' experience over the past six years collaborating with each other and with colleagues to develop, use, and facilitate cases with teachers and other educators. Our colleague Deborah Bryant in particular has been part of the conversation, reflection, and practice that has contributed to shaping the ideas about case facilitation represented here. Our own backgrounds are in professional development and curriculum development as well as in teaching, and we have drawn from these fields in our case work. We understand how educators learn and grow in powerful ways, and see cases as offering the realistic context, challenging issues, and connection to personal experience that supports new insights and ideas. We understand how materials can be crafted to engage educators and address the questions and concerns they have about their practice.

In developing print cases about school reform issues and video cases about curricular and equity issues, we have seen the power of good case facilitation. While we believed in the quality of the print and video cases we developed, we also saw that the real learning came in the engagement of a group with those materials. To that end, facilitation has taken on greater importance. The ideas in this book came from our experience with facilitating cases that we had developed with a variety of groups in very different contexts. We have also facilitated cases that others have developed, and talked and reflected with colleagues who are also engaged in the work of case development and facilitation. Thus, it was our own experience with case facilitation and our efforts to share with others what we had learned that led to this book.

As with most collaborative efforts, it is difficult to trace the particular contributions of each of us, and of Deborah Bryant and others, to this book. However, it particularly reflects Barbara Miller's extensive experience in case facilitation and her thinking about the challenges of planning for and engaging in case experiences with groups. Most of the firsthand experience with facilitation described in this book, including the examples of facilitation that are interspersed throughout, is Barbara's, and much of the book is therefore written by her in the first person. Ilene Kantrov's contributions focused primarily on the ways in which the activities used in the case experience can best be framed and structured to contribute to the successful use of cases. Ilene was also responsible for the initial ideas for the case development work out of which this book grew.

Both of us have been intrigued by the power of good facilitation to support a group in learning in deep ways, and we believe that a book like this can help others develop those kinds of facilitation skills. We also take delight in being able to talk about both what good facilitation entails, and why certain strategies and skills contribute to good facilitation. Writing this book has been an opportunity to work in that enviable intersection of theory and practice. Furthermore, this book pulls together many of the ideas, recommendations, and value statements that previously had existed only in conversations, marginal comments, or memos.

Our case work has been located at Education Development Center, Inc. (EDC), an international nonprofit organization dedicated to promoting human development through education. Founded in 1958, EDC now maintains more than two hundred projects in the United States and throughout the world. The scope of the organization's work reaches from mathematics and science curricula to school health, from environmental education to systemic school reform. EDC specializes in designing and implementing training programs for a wide range of workers and professionals, but particularly for teachers and school administrators.

ACKNOWLEDGMENTS

Many people have helped shape this book in important ways. Deborah Bryant brought her considerable skills in designing professional development work to bear. She offered creative and thoughtful suggestions for framing sections of the manuscript, drew on her own facilitation experience to keep this book connected to the experiences of real people who act as case facilitators, and read with a critical and constructive eye. Leigh Peake has had more than one important role. As acquisitions editor at Heinemann, she convinced us that there was a market for this book and that we were the ones to write it. She was patient throughout the long course of the development of this book, and supportive when it was questionable whether there was the right convergence of time, money, and energy. She was the kind of careful, candid, and constructive reader that every author deserves and few find. Her suggestions on earlier drafts of the manuscript have improved it considerably.

Others have been similarly generous with their ideas and enthusiasm. Joan Karp was an early reader of the manuscript and helped us to think about its application in a wider arena of case work. Grady McGonagill's ideas about effective communication informed our thinking about facilitating case discussions. Natasha Shabat turned our rough sketches into real graphics. Cynthia Grzelcyk provided the necessary administrative support that was key to getting this manuscript out the door and did so with her usual quiet competence. The development of this book was supported, in part, by a grant from The Pew Charitable Trusts.

INTRODUCTION

Cases are tools that are increasingly used in education to explore challenging issues and to reflect on diverse experiences. The most powerful cases are more than narratives of events; they are cases "of something" (L. Shulman 1992, 17). They represent some larger set of ideas and therefore are worthy of reflection and deliberation. A well-crafted case "of something" is like an evocative photograph that captures a subject, invites multiple interpretations, and is rich enough to sustain repeated encounters. Good cases have that same kind of complexity, drawing the reader into the topic and evoking comparisons to other experiences.

A case offers a group a common text for exploring critical education issues. The power of the case is not in the narrative itself, as though the text contained the "answers" or all the essential elements one needs to know to understand an issue. Instead, the power of the case approach is in the use of the case text among the group, in the discussion or experience that is created around the case.

The facilitator, therefore, is critical in accessing the power of cases, to maximize their potential for learning and reflection. This book is an extended discussion of case facilitation, aimed at those who have the charge of using cases to stimulate discussion and reflection. The operating assumption is that cases are being used in a group context, rather than as a tool for solitary reflection, and throughout this book I refer to participants as the members of a group using a case. The discussion of case facilitation offered here focuses on how to structure a "case experience" with such a group of participants. By "case experience" I mean the entire encounter with the group around a particular case.

The case experience is not limited to talking about the case and its issues. The case experience can encompass a range of activities: small and large group exercises, including doing a mathematics or science task as described in a case; silent reflection; and the work that precedes or follows the session in which the group meets to focus on the case. As the facilitator, you are helping to foster an entire professional development experience with a group—not simply leading a group that is talking about a case.

In writing this book, I imagined myself in conversation with you, the case facilitator. As that facilitator, you may be an educator involved in preservice education or professional development with teachers. You may be a university faculty member. You may be a classroom teacher, an administrator, or a central office staff member. You may be someone committed to education working outside of a school or district in a nonprofit, state- or federal-funded position. Regardless of your position, you are curious about how you might facilitate cases to deepen and enrich a group's conversation about educational issues and practice. This book offers both strategies for improving your effectiveness as a facilitator and a conceptual framework for understanding and acting in your role as a facilitator.

WHAT IS A CASE?

Cases have a rich history of use in law, medicine, and business, where they typically provide a detailed context for understanding a particular principle or problem (Kleinfeld 1992; Merseth 1992; Sykes and Bird 1992; Doyle 1990). In education, the term *case* is applied to many different phenomena. To some, it evokes a long, detailed narration of a particular set of events. To others, it means an anthropologically sensitive portrait of an individual or group. To still others, it conveys the twentieth century equivalent of an Aesop's fable. Given this diversity, I want to start with a working definition.

In this book, *case* refers to a narrative organized around a key event and portraying particular characters and that is structured to invite engagement by participants in a discussion of the case. This sort of case is a relatively short text that prompts conversation and reflection on a set of issues that are framed through the narrative. The case does not offer clear and easy answers, and it is structured to be open-ended, inviting a variety of interpretations. Such cases can be used to explore issues, events, and characters that are familiar to discussion participants but provide some distance from "my" issue, "my" event, or "me" as the key player.

Imagine all cases existing along a spectrum. On one end are case studies—in-depth, lengthy descriptions of an individual, event, or institution. There are, for example, a number of case studies of restructured schools describing the ways in which educators have changed their curriculum, assessment, or instruction (for example, see Ames and Miller 1994). On the other end of the spectrum are vignettes— short snippets of action involving a small number of people. An example of this is a brief but provocative description of an interaction between a teacher and student over a grade, a point of information, or an idea raised in discussion (for instance, see Brubaker and Simon 1993 or illustrative examples found in most contemporary university textbooks). The cases that I am talking about fall between these two ends of the case spectrum. They are not as detailed as case studies nor as telegraphic as vignettes. This is because they are not intended to play out the full complexity of an actual event or place, as a case study would. Nor are they meant to illustrate a point, as a vignette does. The cases that I am talking about are sufficiently detailed to promote good discussion and are constructed to address particular issues.

Throughout this book, I refer to one such case, "Oliver's Experiment" (see the appendix). While the story line leads up to the dramatic moment found in many cases ("What should Oliver do next?"), this case is open-ended and constructed to portray a variety of viewpoints about the central issues of alternative assessment and the pace and scope of change in a classroom. Beyond using this particular case as a common text, I also describe my facilitation of "Oliver's Experiment" with a group of high school department chairs and administrators as an extended illustration. I encourage you to take the time to read the case now, since familiarity with it will enhance your understanding of many of the ideas presented here.

WHERE DO YOU FIND CASES?

There is a growing supply of cases in the educational literature. Some of them are cases developed by teachers, capturing particular dimensions of their lives in classrooms and schools. Others have been developed by researchers and developers in university and nonprofit settings for use by teachers and others in exploring a range of issues. Some cases place a greater emphasis on concepts or topics within a particular discipline, like mathematics, science, or English language arts, while other cases focus on issues that cut across disciplines, such as school reform or leadership. (See a list of suggested readings at the end of this book for some of the many casebooks that are available.)

In addition, greater attention is being paid to how teachers and other educators can construct their own cases, thereby adding to the existing stock of cases (see Kleinfeld 1990; J. Shulman 1990; J. Shulman 1992; Merseth 1992; Richert 1992; Wassermann 1993; Schifter 1996). Many of these cases also contain some ideas for using the cases with groups, comparable to the facilitator's guide that accompanies "Oliver's Experiment" (see the appendix).

WHY SHOULD YOU USE CASES?

Within education, cases are used in a variety of contexts. Most often, instructors use cases in teacher education or preservice courses to bring the reality of the classroom into the teacher education curriculum. In addition, instructors use cases in university courses on educational policy and practice to contextualize abstract ideas and theories. Cases offer a window into classrooms, schools, and districts that complements and extends classroom observations, practica, student teaching, or other professional experiences that students in a university setting bring to their studies. In the context of a teacher education or graduate course, cases offer a common text for exploring critical education issues.

Increasingly, cases are used in professional development or inservice contexts, too. With greater emphasis on interactive forms of professional development, cases are an obvious choice to engage teachers in thinking about important educational ideas. As in the teacher education context, a case can be a common text for practicing teachers to consider together. In this way, the case becomes the catalyst for a focused conversation about particular issues, to which teachers can bring their varied experiences to bear.

Across a variety of contexts, the development, use, and facilitation of cases open opportunities to analyze and ponder difficult issues in a particular setting and apply those insights to one's own situation. The power of cases is magnified when they are used in a group setting as a catalyst for discussion. Participants can, in the company of others, engage in analysis of the various problems embedded in the case, work to generate and evaluate alternative solutions, and discuss and reflect upon the underlying issues.

Use of cases in this fashion resembles the kind of good teaching advocated by most current school reform efforts. The call is for teaching that encourages multiple perspectives on a given issue, emphasizes critical thinking, and explores various answers and approaches. When cases are used most productively, they support this kind of teaching and learning. Educators who participate in case discussions experience for themselves the kind of teaching/learning dynamics that they wish for their own classrooms.

A number of educators have posited that the power of cases is greater than their capacity to represent and be responsive to local contexts and concerns. They point to the usefulness of cases in bridging the divide between theory and practice in education, since a case can both embody the reality of education practice and provide evidence of theories in use. In their review of the case literature, Sykes and Bird (1992) described the variety of claims for cases: illustrating instances of theory, rooting abstract ideas in pragmatic action, confronting problems of practice, and exemplifying narrative knowing. Their point is that the "theory into practice" phenomenon is represented differently in these different traditions and is embodied differently in cases. L. Shulman (1987; 1990) and Doyle (1990) both describe how educators can accumulate and construct knowledge through the medium of cases, thereby contributing to theories in use within education. Others (including Merseth 1991 and J. Shulman 1992) emphasize the decision-making dimension of cases, offering educators the opportunity to apply theories to the particular situations portrayed in cases. Despite considerable attention, there is no consensus about the most appropriate or robust theory about the use of cases in education.

Given this diversity of interpretation regarding the interplay between theory and practice within cases, similarly diverse claims are made regarding the effectiveness of cases to promote learning. Education appears to support a wider array of cases than many other fields (Kagan 1993), and therefore many different claims can be made for their effectiveness. The greatest interest, though, seems to be generated by the claim that cases are catalysts that can promote change among educators. The research evidence for this is limited (Kagan 1993; Sykes and Bird 1992; Barnett and Sather 1992), although the commonsense appeal of this claim is evident.

Noting the many different assumptions about the effectiveness of cases and their link to theory, it is vital that those of us writing about cases—their use and facilitation—at least work to make our perspectives on cases explicit. We approach cases as a medium for exploring critical issues within education, emphasizing the capacity of cases to promote discussion and engage a variety of viewpoints. We downplay the use of cases as exemplars to emulate or illustrations to critique, and focus on the ways in which cases function as both windows and mirrors (EDC/EES 1995; Miller, Kantrov, and Hunault 1996). Cases can serve as a *window* into the experiences and ideas of the educators portrayed as they grapple with key issues and as a *mirror* of the beliefs and attitudes of those who read and discuss the case. Participants in a case discussion reflect on and discuss what they see through the window of the case—the actions, issues, and characters that they find engaging. Participants also consider and talk about what they find reflected through the mirror of the case—their own reactions to what they see and what those reactions tell them about themselves and their own circumstances. Working with others, people learn how what appears through the window of the case is reflected differently in others' mirrors. This awareness of difference opens up the possibility of change.

WHAT IS CASE FACILITATION?

To facilitate something is to make a task easier or to assist others in their work. In this book, "case facilitation" refers to the actions of individuals to help others in the group learn from the case experience. The facilitator of a case assists the group engaged in using the case. This happens in two ways. One is by creating a structure that will frame the case for participants (referred to here as "facilitating the case"). Good cases, that is, cases that evoke thoughtful reflection and learning by participants, are like the real-life situations they represent: complex, somewhat messy or ambiguous, and containing elements of the unknown. An important dimension of facilitation is to create a useful structure for discussing the case. The second way in which the case facilitator acts is by engaging the group in its use of the case (referred to here as "facilitating the group"). Any group can benefit from good facilitation to help it achieve its best intentions to be productive and learn from one another. Another important dimension of case facilitation, then, is a game plan and skills for working effectively with groups.

The image I want to create is that of an active, purposeful facilitator. No matter how skilled you are in group management skills or how intimately familiar you are with a particular case, I encourage you to adopt the mindset that case facilitation is a very active role. It means that you need to be clear in your intentions and goals for a particular case and with a particular group, and that you communicate this to participants. In some ways, case facilitation is like the Socratic method of teaching in that you utilize thoughtful questions that provoke deeper reflection on the part of participants. In some ways, case facilitation is like good coaching in that you are mindful of and drawing upon the ideas and strengths of the participants. With both of these comparisons, you are called upon to be purposeful in your actions.

Case facilitation is not, in my opinion, like being a traffic cop. While this is an image of facilitation in other contexts, where the goal is to keep the conversational traffic flowing and to maximize the number of people who are able to share their ideas, this is not the ideal with case facilitation. True, you do want to encourage participants to talk.

However, the goal is not to have the maximum number of comments passing through the traffic circle known as the case discussion. Rather, you want to be able to do something with those ideas and to create an experience in which all are participants and not merely vehicles passing through the intersection.

The role of facilitator may be an explicit one, as in groups where someone is assigned to, volunteers for, or is recruited to take on facilitation responsibilities on behalf of the group. The role of facilitator may be more implicit, as with groups in which an individual takes on leadership responsibilities with the tacit support of other members. In this book I advocate that the role of case facilitator be made explicit and public. The group needs to know who the facilitator is and understand his/her responsibilities. Similarly, the facilitator needs to possess some skill and confidence in assisting the group to learn from the case experience. The approach to case facilitation presented here articulates ways in which facilitators can develop their capacity and confidence to assist groups to learn from cases.

This approach takes a point of view. It is not a generic approach to facilitation, although much of what is said here applies to a wide variety of cases. This approach to case facilitation focuses on analysis and inquiry, and the skills presented here are most likely to be effective when used to achieve those goals. From this perspective, good case facilitation is rooted in the capacity of the facilitator to build a rich analysis of the case and its issues through inquiry into participants' perspectives about the case and about their own experience. This approach is summed up by five goals of facilitation that are described here and are the foundation for the skills and strategies presented in this book:

- Focus on analysis over evaluation.
- Promote inquiry into different perspectives.
- Refrain from problem solving too quickly.
- Build common understanding.
- Adopt a learning stance.

Focus on Analysis over Evaluation

As facilitator, your goal is to help participants stay focused on exploring the many layers of ideas that a good case contains. Keep the emphasis on exploration, because you will then help participants work from an analytic rather than an evaluative stance. Compare this approach to an archeological expedition. As an archeologist uncovers a site, she concentrates on what can be learned from each layer of artifacts. To this task she brings analytic skills—considering what the relation is between various bits, wondering about the relative placement of different objects, developing theories about the meaning of assorted articles. As a case facilitator, you are similarly focused on bringing your analytic skills to understanding the issues in a case and to making sense of the perspectives and interpretations that participants bring to the case. You and the participants are joined in this expedition, inquiring together about what can be learned from a given case.

This focus on analysis is different from a focus on evaluation. As facilitator, you are working to guide participants away from a more familiar stance of critique: What is right or wrong in the case? What is good or bad in the characters' actions? What is to be emulated or rejected in the strategies used? In general, we are more used to evaluating narratives of practice than analyzing them. We are more experienced in applying often unstated criteria about a "right" or "wrong" answer, a "good" or "bad" response, so it is natural that we would bring that approach to cases as well.

Let's return to the archeology metaphor. Taking an evaluative stance, an archeologist would be looking at each layer, at every artifact, for the purpose of making judgments about the people who left this record. Were they an advanced civilization? Were they innovative? As an archeologist, she has a point of view and is capable of making evaluative judgments. However, the evaluation of quality, of rightness/wrongness, goodness/badness, is not the stance that an archeologist typically takes, at least not until careful analysis has taken place, because an evaluative stance often precludes deeper inquiry. It is tempting to stick with the surface, what is easily seen and understood, and draw conclusions based on that. It is more difficult to dig beneath the surface, whether we are archeologists or educators, to analyze a case in order to look closely at the issues raised and to ponder their meaning *in situ* as well as for ourselves.

This distinction between analysis and evaluation can be illustrated in the facilitation of "Oliver's Experiment." As the facilitator, I could elicit judgments from participants about Oliver's actions. Did he do the right thing by trying a new unit? by experimenting with new forms of assessment? by sharing his concerns with Mrs. Ramirez? These questions lead to interesting conversations with participants, inviting them to evaluate the usefulness of Oliver's choices. They can, though, lead to superficial conversations if they are not grounded in some analysis of Oliver's actions and motivations. By focusing primarily on evaluation, you enable participants to make evaluations, and sometimes sweeping evaluations at that, without grounding them in careful analysis. By focusing on analysis, at least as a precursor to evaluation, you help participants articulate their perspectives on Oliver's actions, his reasons for acting, and the implications of those choices. You keep the emphasis on understanding what Oliver did and why, a move that in the long run is more likely to elicit participants' deeply held perspectives, not only to invite their judgments about Oliver's choices.

Promote Inquiry into Different Perspectives

Discussing and studying cases with a group of people offers the opportunity to encounter a variety of perspectives. For many, a case can act as a kind of projective device, almost like a Rorschach test, into which participants read their own experiences, concerns, and ideas. In this way, cases are fertile ground for eliciting different perspectives from participants, and an important goal for you is to create an environment in which different perspectives can be articulated and considered.

Different people, because of their different experiences, make different sense of the world and different meaning from a case text. As a facilitator, you too bring your own perspective to the case and the group of participants. Promoting inquiry into different perspectives means developing awareness of the assumptions and values that you bring to your work as a facilitator. You need to be willing to test out your assumptions about the group and its ideas, and to acknowledge your values about issues in the case as perhaps different from those of others, in order to listen for and ask about others' perspectives.

By promoting inquiry into different perspectives, you can help participants build awareness of their own points of view and the ways in which those ideas serve and limit them. Developing the capacity to see how our assumptions and values shape the meaning we make of cases, and how our perspectives might limit what we understand, is a valuable skill. As a facilitator, you can help participants acquire this skill by promoting inquiry into different perspectives. Sometimes we mistake our own perspective for "the truth." We don't realize that others understand a case differently, or see an alternative strategy, or value another action, unless we can hear those ideas and work to understand them.

For example, in facilitating "Oliver's Experiment" with a variety of different groups, I have heard a wide range of perspectives expressed about Bill, the department chair in the case. Some participants have dismissed Bill as ineffective in his capacity as department chair. Others have viewed him as obstructionist, actively working to prevent Oliver from making necessary changes in his classroom practice. Still others are sympathetic to Bill and describe him as being in a tough position, mediating among teachers like Oliver, administrators, and parents such as Mrs. Ramirez. Others applaud Bill for advocating for reform and supporting alternative assessment in his department. Some are just plain confused by Bill, don't quite know what to make of him in the context of the case, and characterize Bill himself as inconsistent. Who is right? Who has the accurate reading of this character?

Each of these perspectives on Bill is "right," in that each one conveys the views of particular participants. Rather than engaging in a contest of wills ("I have the best interpretation of Bill and his motivations"), as the facilitator you can invite participants to share their various views of this character as the first step toward inquiring further into their own perspectives. Inquiry into different perspectives means investigating the underlying assumptions and values that each person carries about who Bill is and what Bill should do. Your role is to help participants explore and articulate impressions of a character like Bill in order to give other participants access to generally unstated ideas. Making those unstated and implicit ideas public will enrich the discussion. Moreover, as the facilitator, you want to elicit a variety of perspectives, since it is often by contrast that we can see differences. Hearing only a single perspective about Bill ("He's ineffective") does little to open up conversation. Working with a variety of perspectives ("Some say Bill is ineffective, others say he is an advocate for reform, and one person says he's caught in a tough position") offers participants, and you, the chance to dig more deeply into the underlying values about a particular character or issue in a case.

Refrain from Problem Solving Too Quickly

Many people approach cases as puzzles to be solved, and invest a good deal of energy in determining the best solution. Many cases are structured so as to suggest a particular solution as the most productive course of action. However, engaging in a case only to solve the problem misses much of the power of a case.

When people approach a case as a problem to be solved, they are likely assuming that the problem is a given and therefore known by everyone. Yet, most often, this is not so. What Regina sees as the problem in the case could be quite different from what Ted sees as the problem in the case. So, if Regina moves to solve the problem she sees without defining it or developing some agreement in the group about its nature, she runs the risk of working solo, since the problem she sees and the problem that Ted or anyone else in group sees are often different. Defining the problem in the case is a critical aspect of the case experience and can be the richest part of the discussion. Understanding what other participants see as the problem in the case—and why they understand it as problematic—leads to deeper understanding of the issues.

Therefore, I suggest that, as facilitator, you refrain from problem solving too quickly and that you work with participants to moderate their desire to jump into a problem-solving mode. Opening up the case so that participants can consider different problems, and therefore pursue a variety of solutions, means that you and the participants can delve more deeply into the issues and move beyond the puzzle that may be present only on the surface of the case. It's not that you should never engage in problem solving. Rather, view problem solving as a multistage process in which problem definition is as important as generating solutions to the problem.

One of the study questions posed at the end of "Oliver's Experiment" is a query common in case discussions: What should Oliver do next? I have witnessed lively debates among participants passionately advocating a particular solution for Oliver ("I think he should continue to experiment in his classroom and not be held back by people like Bill or Mrs. Ramirez." "What are you talking about?! Oliver needs to take stock of his options, and his best option is to get Bill on his side and patch things up with Mrs. Ramirez. He doesn't know enough yet to be experimenting on his students.") While I always hope that a case discussion generates passion and involvement on the part of participants, these debates about what Oliver should do next can quickly devolve into an argument in which the "winner" is the one who speaks the loudest and longest.

If getting to the solution as expeditiously as possible is viewed as the primary goal of a case discussion, you will lose much of the learning potential in a case. Refraining from problem solving too quickly means spending time articulating what a problem is in the case, testing out participants' interpretations of the magnitude or meaning of that problem, and then moving to generating and analyzing various solutions. Given the nature of the complex human problems addressed in cases, there is no completely objective point from which anyone—you or participants—can argue for the veracity of a particular solution. You want to help participants understand the nature of the problems inherent in the case so that you all can be more informed as you consider various solutions.

Build Common Understanding

In the case experience, you can build a common understanding with participants about the issues and ideas in a particular case. You take advantage of a fundamental characteristic of a case: it establishes an equivalent distance from the events for all participants. In a personal story, the teller has authority. It's his experience and he is in the position of framing it so as to emphasize his interpretation of events. In a case, no one participant has that authority. While good cases resonate with participants' own experience and often generate comments such as "I'm just like Oliver!" this is different from working with a personal story. Given that all participants have more or less equal access to the case, you have a good opportunity to build a common understanding about the issues implicit in that case.

As the facilitator, you want to help participants move beyond an exchange of opinions into consideration of what it is that you, as a group, are learning together from the case. Case discussion runs the risk of only being a forum for educators to swap experiences ("Oh, this case is just like something that happened a couple of years ago. Let me tell you about it."). While educators need more opportunities to share their experiences, there is a greater need to analyze and inquire into those experiences in order to learn more than what happened to one individual in a particular situation.

When you approach a case as the opportunity to build a common understanding, you take as your charge the work of developing a shared understanding about a set of issues that is greater than the aggregation of often disparate comments from the group. Your task as facilitator is to help synthesize what the group is exploring and articulate the larger ideas that emerge. This does not mean that you will arrive at complete agreement. In fact, a critical aspect of building a common understanding may be uncovering and naming the very real differences in opinion among group participants. You want to work to help the group focus on the issues of greatest importance, whether or not there is complete agreement regarding chapter and verse.

This is not the work of a neutral, dispassionate facilitator. Often, how you as a facilitator build this common understanding is by bringing your own ideas into the discussion, offering them to the group as an avenue—though not the only way—to build a common understanding. Your views become part of that understanding, without substituting for it.

As I facilitated "Oliver's Experiment" with a group of administrators and high school department chairs, I was working to build a common understanding about the critical issues in the case for this group. We ended up naming assessment as a critical driver for change in classroom practice for Oliver and probably for his school. The group did not completely agree about how change in classroom practice should proceed, nor did I think that such agreement was critical. My charge was to develop a common understanding of assessment and to keep that as our focus for discussion.

Adopt a Learning Stance

Case facilitation is a learning opportunity, so that participants and you can end the case experience knowing more about and understanding more deeply the issues presented in the case and, most likely, knowing more about one another. In analyzing a case with a group, and actively soliciting and working to understand different perspectives, you are adopting a learning stance. As a facilitator, you see yourself leaving the case experience with new ideas, fresh insights, a wider set of experiences—with more than when you began the case experience. As a facilitator, you need to bring a healthy curiosity to the case. What am I wondering about regarding the case itself? this group's understanding of the issues? a particular idea? This curiosity guides the case experience.

Of course, you are always involved in negotiating trade-offs in your role as facilitator. You cannot pursue every idea that is presented, nor can you explore every question you or participants may have. So you cannot bring an all-encompassing curiosity to the case; you cannot learn everything that may be possibly learned from a case—and certainly not in one session! However, by adopting a learning stance, you are more likely to approach a case open to new ideas for yourself and encouraging participants in their attempts to explore, analyze, and inquire. Moreover, you are helping participants make sense for themselves, and for the group, of the case and its issues rather than bearing the sole responsibility yourself.

Thus, you want participants also to adopt a learning stance in the case experience. Through your facilitation, you can aid them in this effort. By focusing more on what participants are wondering about or are trying to understand more deeply, and concentrating less on what participants know in an unquestioning way, you can set the stage for their professional learning and growth. In a good case experience, everyone in some way learns something through the discussion of and reflection about the case. You have the chance to help develop participants' capacity to adopt a learning stance by modeling for them inquiry into and analysis of the case.

In facilitating "Oliver's Experiment," one of the bigger challenges I face is promoting a learning stance. It is much easier for participants to come to the case ready to confirm what they already believe and advocate for what they already know. A participant might state, with great conviction born from personal experience, that "in a situation like this, the best thing that Oliver can do is to cut his losses and come back to fight another day. Once Mrs. Ramirez sees him as experimenting on her kid, he's not going to win." This could be a new point of view for another participant, and therefore a source of learning. But has the participant voicing this sentiment learned anything new? I don't think so. What, then, might this participant learn from the case? Perhaps, the participant might explore how Oliver's situation is different from her personal experience, or take a close look at some of the assumptions that led to her assurance about "the best thing that Oliver can do."

It takes more energy for all of us—participants and facilitator—to be in a learning frame of mind, looking for new insights and new ways of thinking about the situation. Through my facilitation of a case, particularly by modeling the ways in which I look for new ideas in the case experience, I can help participants adopt a learning stance. By encouraging participants to talk about what they are wondering about in a case and to pursue questions or hunches they have, I can help them explore different options. When I call attention to a statement like "Once Mrs. Ramirez sees him as experimenting on her kid, he's not going to win," I open up the chance for everyone to look closely at what is meant by experimentation and how honoring parents' real concerns for their children's achievement is weighed against the equally real need for teachers to grow and change in their classroom practice. By not staying with the pronouncement about the "best thing that Oliver can do" and instead exploring what is behind such a statement, I am at least opening up the chance for the participant who voiced this opinion to learn more about what she meant and why it meant so much to her. At the same time, I am inviting other participants to learn more about this point of view and about their own ideas, too.

OVERVIEW OF THIS BOOK

This book considers both how to facilitate cases and how to think about case facilitation. I know that there is great merit in being specific about strategies and moves that make for effective case facilitation, and I have tried to do so throughout. My hope is that you develop a clear image of what you might do when you facilitate by considering the ideas presented here. At the same time, I don't believe that case facilitation should be like following a recipe, no matter how complicated that recipe might be. I am presenting a framework for facilitation, encouraging you to be purposeful in your choices as facilitator. To that end, I have presented particular strategies and moves in light of that framework.

As a case facilitator, there are some specific things you can attend to that will improve the case experience for participants and for you. As noted earlier, I distinguish between two kinds of facilitation: facilitating the case and facilitating the group, discussed in Chapters 2 and 3, respectively. In terms of facilitating the case, your focus is on the case itself—the story and the issues raised—and the ways it connects with the group you are working with. Facilitating the case is about framing the issues in ways that are accessible to and engaging for participants. Much of this work occurs prior to the actual interaction with participants, as you develop a structure or a plan for the case experience that will guide participants in exploring, reflecting upon, and learning from the case.

In facilitating the group, your focus is on the work of eliciting and learning from the variety of perspectives participants in the group bring to the case experience. You are attending to the group itself—the experiences and points of view of its members, and the ways they connect with the case and each other. Much of this work occurs during the case experience, as you monitor group dynamics, lead discussion, synthesize ideas, and engage in other activities that make for a coherent and focused learning experience.

Facilitating the case and facilitating the group are certainly interrelated tasks. By asking you to focus on them as separate activities, I highlight the importance of attending closely to the case and what it has to offer and then attending closely to the group and what its members have to offer. The case experience is an opportunity for powerful learning when both parts—the case and the group—are in sync. A case, no matter how compelling because of its appealing characters, dramatic story line, or challenging issues, is more powerful when the discussion is an interplay between the case text and the perspectives, expectations, and ideas of the participants in the group. As the facilitator, it is easy for you to become too focused on one or another dimension of facilitation. The case may be challenging for you, so you spend most of your energy understanding it. Or the group may be new to you, so you spend most of your time focused on the participants. However, effective case facilitation demands that you not forsake one kind of facilitation for the other. Both are important; both deserve attention.

Following the discussion of facilitating the case and facilitating the group is a chapter on managing your concerns as a facilitator. You bring a variety of ideas, experiences, expectations, and mindsets to the role of case facilitator. It is useful, therefore, to look closely at the concerns you have about playing this role, with an eye toward managing them in ways that will help you be more productive and confident in your facilitation work. Part of what is demanding about case facilitation is that, as the facilitator, your skills and credibility are on display for all to see. Part of the satisfaction and growth that can come from case facilitation is developing your skills and increasing your credibility, in your eyes as well as in the eyes of participants. Yet, I know that the proof is in the pudding. What is important is that you actually facilitate a case, whether you are a novice or a veteran. This book is meant to support individuals new to case facilitation as well as those who have been doing it for a number of years. For both, I think this book will offer a useful way to reflect on the work of case facilitation.

Throughout the book, as in this introduction, I refer frequently to "Oliver's Experiment" (see the appendix). In order to make the discussion of case facilitation more grounded, I have drawn many examples from my (and colleagues') facilitation of this case. "Oliver's Experiment" is a case that I know well, since I was involved in its development and have facilitated its use with many different groups of people. It is a case that I continue to be challenged by and learn more about every time I facilitate it with a different group. In this book, I often draw examples from my facilitation of "Oliver's Experiment" with a particular group of high school department chairs and administrators. In addition, I describe some alternative decisions that I have made in facilitating the case with other groups to illustrate further what goes into constructing a plan of work around a particular case.

My close association with this case is both a strength and a weakness. I know the case well and therefore can use it to illustrate a number of points. At the same time, because I know the case so well, I have to work hard to recognize the different ways in which participants make sense of the case and to listen closely for what they value and wonder about. I've tried to convey some of that challenge in this book, too. I want you to be able to use "Oliver's Experiment" as a tool for understanding and exploring the ideas presented here. If you haven't already, I strongly encourage you to read the case narrative now, review the facilitator's guide for the case, and then, as you read this book, consider how the various strategies discussed play out in the context of "Oliver's Experiment".

At the end of the book is a list of suggested readings. The suggested readings include casebooks and facilitator's guides that I have used in my work. This is by no means a complete list. I know that others who facilitate cases will have selections to add to the list. It is, though, a resource for engaging in the work of case facilitation.

2

FACILITATING THE CASE

In facilitating a case, your attention is on what the particular case has to offer you and the participants you are working with. You want to frame issues in the case so that participants will be able to access and explore them. But how to use cases, particularly open-ended cases that invite discussion and reflection (like "Oliver's Experiment") is not obvious in the structure of the cases themselves. Even if you are working with a facilitator's guide or other kinds of notes for a case, you need to develop a game plan for how you want to use and facilitate the case with a particular group of participants. In this chapter, I describe an approach for developing that game plan. The approach has three parts: doing advance planning, structuring the case experience, and making strategic decisions. Each part is described separately in order to highlight what is unique or distinctive about each one, although in reality they operate in a recursive fashion.

Imagine that these three parts are actually three loops of a spiral that start out wide and get progressively more narrow (see Figure 2.1). The first and largest loop is doing advance planning, which casts a rather wide net and may well capture more information or ideas than you can use. The second, smaller loop is more focused, as you make decisions about how you will develop a structure for the time spent with participants. Finally, the third loop is even tighter and more focused, as you make strategic decisions that fine-tune the structure of the case experience. A facilitator doesn't move through these three loops in lockstep. Describing the activities in a linear fashion, though, gives me the opportunity to focus attention on the different kinds of concerns a facilitator needs to attend to in facilitating a case.

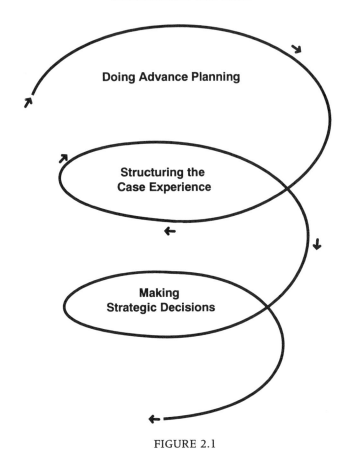

FIGURE 2.1

In this and subsequent chapters I make reference to my own facilitation of "Oliver's Experiment" with a group of department chairs and administrators from one high school and talk about the decisions I made in facilitating this case. A little background information about this group and its interests will set the stage for how I made decisions about facilitating the case in this context.

This group of seventeen consisted of teachers who acted as chairs of departments of all the disciplines at the high school, along with school administrators and special program directors. This group had met regularly in the past and had taken up the charge of investigating alternative assessment approaches that could be used across the entire school. This group had developed a rapport that encouraged lively conversation and thoughtful reflection. A member of the group contacted me about working with them to look at alternative assessment, and I suggested "Oliver's Experiment" as a good tool for addressing their needs.

DOING ADVANCE PLANNING

Advance planning is the work that you, as a facilitator, undertake before you put together the agenda for a case discussion. Think of this as the preparation work that goes on in a restaurant kitchen, prior to the assembly and serving of the individual dishes. The menu reflects the tastes of the chef and, hopefully, those of the customers. The kitchen preparation needs to happen in a timely fashion, and the dishes need to be in some state of readiness, even though each may not be served on that day. So, too, with advance planning for a case. Even though you, as the facilitator, may not use all of what you've prepared, you need to be in a state of readiness with the activities (dishes) you selected for the case experience (meal).

There are four different tasks that I recommend you do as part of your advance planning (see Figure 2.2):

- Know the participants.
- Select and know the case.
- Articulate goals.
- "Translate" if necessary.

To extend the restaurant analogy, knowing the participants is comparable to having a good idea of your restaurant clientele and their preferences. Knowing the case is like becoming very familiar with the kinds of ingredients you are working with. Articulating goals is like creating a menu, particularly one that may change seasonally or over time. "Translating" is appreciating that some diners may be unfamiliar with radicchio or chili paste and helping to educate their palates.

Know the Participants

The maxim "know your audience" is applicable to case facilitation. You must have a good understanding of the experiences and expectations that participants will bring to the case discussion. The more you know about the participants and what they will bring, the more material you, as a facilitator, will have to work with. This may be information that you, as the facilitator, already have because of your past interactions with the participants, or it may be information that others have provided. Alternatively, you may need to do some inquiry of your own into what participants will be bringing to the discussion.

You may need to gather information about the participants in order to select a case that will best meet their needs. Knowing about them will help you choose a case that can challenge their ideas or ex-

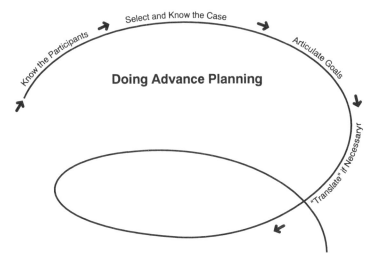

FIGURE 2.2

tend their thinking, not merely replicate their experience. Or you may be weighing the interests of the participants against the potential of a particular case for engaging them in reflective conversation. To that end, you can draw on your knowledge of the case and ask about the presence of the case issues in the experiences of the participants. You can check into the similarity between the case and the educational world in which participants live and work. You can ask about the participants' current professional concerns, since those will most likely be reflected in the discussion of the case regardless of the expressed purpose. The bottom line is that you, as the facilitator, need to assess the group and develop working hypotheses about what it will bring to the table as you enter into discussion of the case.

By talking with the individual who was arranging for the case discussion, I learned that the department chairs and administrators with whom I would be working had a long-standing relationship, since most of them had been teaching at the school for a number of years. They were also educators who had worked together on alternative assessment over the past year, exploring different discipline-based strategies for changing the kinds of assessment used to measure students' learning. They were familiar enough with different kinds of alternative assessment to be raising critical questions about implementation and impact. They were thinking about how teachers and parents would respond to changes in assessment. As a group, they needed to reach consensus over the next few months about what kinds of alternative assessment they would recommend to their colleagues and to the community.

My knowledge of the participants and their interests led me to formulate a hypothesis about what they would bring to a case like "Oliver's Experiment." I anticipated that they would be focused on implementation issues and approach "Oliver's Experiment" as an illustration of "what happens when"—in this case, what happens when a classroom teacher begins to change homework and tests to reflect a changing pedagogy—and be interested in exploring how various characters interpret these kinds of changes.

Select and Know the Case

Knowing the participants influences which case you choose to work with, or how you frame a particular case for a given group. The case is a tool for building an engaging and reflective discussion with participants, and you want to use it as effectively as you can. Given what I had learned about the participants, I saw "Oliver's Experiment" as a good case to use with this group. While the major themes of the case as originally written focused on the process of change for a classroom teacher when he began to experiment with new curriculum and assessment, I felt that the assessment issues were accessible enough for the case to promote a good discussion.

"Oliver's Experiment" seemed like a good selection for this group on two counts. First, the case connected with the particular questions that the participants currently had about the ramifications of changing assessment, and responded to their needs as they articulated them at this time. Second, the case set those questions and needs against the larger backdrop of alternative assessment and the pace and scope of classroom change.

Beyond selecting the case, an important dimension of advance planning is knowing the case text well enough so that you don't have to rely on extensive notes to navigate through the story or raise the important issues during discussion. The facilitator's guide or case notes that accompany most cases will be of help here, but more important is your own reading and reflecting on the case. Read the case a few times. Take time to identify any terms that may be unfamiliar to you or, more important, any elements of the case that challenge your own ideas. Consider the distinctive features of the case. If chronology is an important feature of the case, know the chronology. If the cast of characters speak to different issues, know the characters. If the case raises a number of issues, know the array of possible issues. In short, do your homework on the case so that you can use it as a tool in discussion, not as the sole focus of conversation.

"Oliver's Experiment" is a case I know well, since I was involved in its development. Nevertheless, I read the case a few times, thinking about what was distinctive, given the group of department chairs and administrators with whom I would be working. The first scene, involving Oliver and a parent, Mrs. Ramirez, would be particularly interesting to these participants, since one of their long-term goals was communicating changes in policies to parents. I also thought that the interaction between Oliver and Bill, the department chair, would pique the interest of the participants, given their own roles within their departments.

I knew that my own interest in the case was focused more on the process of change that Oliver underwent as he rethought and reworked elements of his own practice, and that I had usually paid most attention to the first scene, between Oliver and Mrs. Ramirez, and the last scene, in which Oliver and Bill think about issues of change. I needed to look more closely at these scenes with the interests of the present participants in mind. I began to reflect on a few questions: How is assessment, and changing classroom practice around assessment, experienced by Oliver? by the parent, Mrs. Ramirez? by the department chair, Bill? How do the experiences of these characters begin to open up the issue of assessment for this group?

Articulate Goals

Knowing the participants and selecting and knowing the case are not enough advance preparation for effective case facilitation. You also need to articulate your goals. Why are you using the case? What outcomes do you seek from the case experience? Cases can be used, and therefore facilitated, for a number of purposes, so it is vital that you, as a facilitator, be clear in your own mind and negotiate with participants the purpose of the case discussion. You can have more than one goal or purpose for a case but, again, you need to be clear about what they are. Some of the more commonly identified goals for case discussion are to

- Define and solve problems
- Learn about ideas
- Extract principles
- Plan actions

These goals are certainly connected in many ways, yet a focus on one over the other will have implications for the structure of the case experience in terms of discussion, activities, and your actions as a facilitator.

I can illustrate the distinctions among these various goals in reference to "Oliver's Experiment." I could use "Oliver's Experiment" to define problems, for example, alignment problems that arise when teachers change a particular aspect of their practice. Here, the aim would be to articulate the various dimensions of the problem, such as the impact a new curriculum has on old assessment approaches or the implications of one teacher's new practices for colleagues in the department. I would be trying to uncover assumptions about what the "real" problem is. Having defined a problem, I could then work with the group to try to solve the problem posed. Problem solving is the most familiar purpose for cases. For example, the problem might be framed as, What should Oliver do to communicate more effectively with Leti and her mother? Using the information and ideas presented in the case, I might work with participants to construct some possible solutions to the problem of communication about policy changes, particularly concerning alternative assessment.

Alternatively, I might use "Oliver's Experiment" because I wanted to create a forum in which participants might learn about ideas, such as the scope and pace of change in a teacher's practice. This case would offer a common context to think and learn about the ramifications of implementing change quickly or slowly, broadly or in a more focused manner. I could also use the case to focus on a different idea, namely, the implications of alternative assessment for teachers, department chairs, students, and parents. Here, the case would be a shared text to reflect on alternative assessment and its impact in a school community.

Another purpose for using this case might be to extract principles to apply in other situations. I might use "Oliver's Experiment" to determine the necessary conditions for successful implementation of new kinds of classroom assessment and, from this case, generate some principles to try out in other situations. The discussion might focus on elements that we think are critical to assessment change, considering how applicable these elements might be in a middle school or elementary school setting, or in a discipline other than mathematics.

A still different goal is to use "Oliver's Experiment" to plan actions. I might ask participants to describe the various steps that Oliver could take to build greater coherence between his curriculum and assessment practices, creating a kind of blueprint for change that could be applicable in other situations. The focus then would be to develop a plan for change that extends beyond the case, attending to concerns such as resources and support networks.

These same kinds of goals for case discussion apply in other, more content-focused cases. A case that features a group of high school students working together on a physics experiment, or a teacher and her middle school students discussing a challenging mathematics problem involving proportional reasoning, can serve the same range of goals. As the facilitator, you might use the mathematics case to define and solve problems (identifying and overcoming common arithmetic errors student make in proportional reasoning problems); learn about ideas (investigating proportional reasoning as a mathematical construct); extract principles (determining different kinds of approaches students take with proportional reasoning problems and comparing these to approaches used with other kinds of problems); or plan actions (developing follow-up lessons to build students' understanding of proportional reasoning).

Each of these goals for using a case is worthwhile, and any one of them would make for a lively discussion. However, these goals (not to mention others that could be identified) are different from one another. Structuring the case experience to extract principles is a different undertaking than structuring it to define and solve problems or learn about ideas. Given sufficient time with the case and the group, you might achieve many, if not all, of these goals. However, most facilitators will not have that kind of time. It is vital, therefore, to be selective and explicit about the goal (or even the two goals) for using the case, since that goal will guide your choice of discussion questions and activities. It will determine the kinds of outcomes participants might expect by the end of the case experience. It will shape the kind of work you, as a facilitator, will engage in when working with the case with participants.

As a facilitator, you need a clear understanding of the goal for using the case. However, you aren't the sole arbiter of the goal. This needs to be a decision that, minimally, is informed by what you know about the group's expectations, past experiences, and interests. Ideally, the goal is negotiated with at least some of the participants. Through conversation with some of the participants prior to the case discussion, you can hypothesize about the purpose of the case and get input from a few people, or you can ask for feedback from the group at the beginning of the discussion.

You need to take into account the interests expressed by participants. At the same time, you need to advocate for a goal that you believe will best serve the group. These aren't always consistent, at the outset, and part of your role is to test out the fit between what the group identifies as a goal and what you advocate as a goal. Regardless of how the decision is made, the group should know the intended goal(s) for using a particular case.

In the situation noted earlier, where I was using "Oliver's Experiment" with a group of high school department chairs and administrators, articulating the goal was a bit tricky. The group's interest, as represented by one member with whom I spoke ahead of time, was to get on with the work of planning how to implement new assessment changes and how to bring teachers and parents on board. The goal the group members wanted to pursue with the case was to plan actions. They hoped, in a sense, to learn from Oliver's mistakes and to plan for a more successful assessment implementation.

In talking with individuals in the group, I learned about their earlier efforts on assessment. They had already looked at grading practices across the school, as a way to grapple with the larger issue of what they wanted students to know and be able to do as they entered the twenty-first century. They had been involved in other large-scale change efforts involving new curriculum implementation and were also mindful of the challenges of changing classroom practice. The group would be looking at assessment issues and the implications of changing to alternative forms of assessment over the course of the school year, and this case was one of its first activities for the year. Still, many in the group felt that they needed to embark quickly on action planning in order to implement new assessment changes.

As I learned more about this particular group and its efforts on assessment, I wondered how much its members had talked together about their own understanding of alternative assessment. In the pressured environment of schools, reflection can feel like a dispensable commodity in the face of implementation challenges. However, without a clear, shared understanding of the issue, these department chairs and administrators would be sorely hampered in their work of advocating for assessment changes with colleagues and parents. They would have a tough time building buy-in for new assessment policies and helping colleagues change assessment practices if they themselves weren't in agreement about the meaning and importance of alternative assessment for their district. As a way to develop that understanding in the group, I articulated a different goal for the case, namely, to use the case to learn more about alternative assessment and the kinds of changes it demands in classrooms and schools. The goal of planning actions to implement assessment change was important but, for this group, seemed premature. Given that these participants had a year to work on assessment, beginning with a solid, shared understanding of the issue and the kinds of changes it entails seemed like a good investment for them.

I talked with the representative of the group, and we discussed the gap between the group's implied goal and the goal for which I was advocating. As the facilitator, this was my chance to articulate why and how I believed the goal of learning about an idea could serve the group better than its goal of planning actions. I understood the group's concerns but disagreed with the way it wanted to handle them. The group representative agreed with my assessment of the situation and suggested goal, and I went on to plan the case experience with the goal of learning more about assessment and the challenges such a change poses within the school and community. At the beginning of the case experience, when I met with the full group, I described this goal to the participants and reviewed my understanding of their interests. They agreed that implementation was a pressing concern, were willing to spend some time looking at the issue of assessment, but wanted to get to a place in the discussion where they could at least generate some ideas about how to plan for implementation. I suspected that the goal of learning about the issue would offer some new angles for their sub-sequent planning work, so this seemed like a good idea to me, too.

As the facilitator, you want to be in the position where you can articulate and advocate for particular goal(s) for using the case. This is a critical part of the advance planning that you need to do. Think about your advance planning as finding a balance between what the participants are interested in and what you would like accomplish. If you are working with a good case—one that is complex and realistic—it will support a wide variety of goals. Your task is to negotiate between what the participants want to do and what you are advocating to do with the case, to find a good balance point. Finding a good balance point takes some work; it is not a matter of finding the halfway point between your goals and the group's goals.

In using "Oliver's Experiment" with these department chairs and administrators, I was working to balance their interest in implementa-tion issues with my focus on learning more about alternative assess-ment. I had to understand the substance of their interests and take them into account as I advocated for a learning goal for the group. I had to offer a rationale for this particular goal and to frame it so that all parties—participants and facilitator—felt that their interests were at least acknowledged, if not addressed directly.

There is no magic formula that specifies how this negotiation hap-pens. Keep in mind that you need to be clear about what goal you be-lieve would best help the group to learn, and that this goal must reflect what you have learned about the group and its interests. It is your re-sponsibility to "make a case" for a particular goal in the case experience.

"Translate" if Necessary

You may need to do some "translation" of the case text as a part of your advance planning. Translating the case text means making sure that the vocabulary used is understood by participants, seeing that the characters and circumstances portrayed in the case are familiar enough without triggering associations you may not want to deal with in dis-cussion, and ensuring that issues are framed in ways that are accessible to the group. I recommend that you tackle the task of translation only after you have done the work of getting to know the group, getting to know the case, and articulating goals. Your choice of what terms to define, what context setting to do with participants, or what pieces of the text to adapt should be based on your earlier advance planning. Otherwise, any "translation" you do might end up masking—from you or from participants—your goals for the case.

Keep in mind that most good cases have been carefully crafted and that it's easy to create unintended problems as you try to "fix" something else. Without going overboard, there may be particular places where you want to do some translation. Consider how accessible the case text is to participants, and begin by thinking of this in the most basic, literal sense. Some cases provide a glossary of terms or concepts that may be unfamiliar to participants. If one is not provided, you might want to construct one. In the case of "Oliver's Experiment," it is necessary to explain what is meant by Oliver's colleague, Lucy, being off-track. This term refers to the period of time when a subset of teachers and students are not in school, and is usually used in districts where schools are open year round. It is not, as some participants in a discussion of the case once speculated, a euphemism for a nervous breakdown, an interpretation that would lead to a very different set of conclusions about the issues in the case!

In some cases, the glossary is not sufficient. The participants need a deeper understanding of the context of the case to help frame the discussion. Some cases offer background information about the case, or you might know more about the setting or circumstances of the case. This information may be useful in explaining some aspect of the case that is unfamiliar to participants (like year-round schools in which a teacher is off-track). What is more likely, though, is that participants want to know more details about the circumstances portrayed in the case or the characters' backgrounds, actions, and motivations. You can share the ways in which participants in other discussions have interpreted the context, you can offer your own elaboration on the case text, or you can inquire into why knowing certain details is important to participants. Whether you offer more context or not, participants will add details themselves or extrapolate from the text. You need to understand what additional context setting they desire or are creating on their own in order to have a productive discussion using the case. (This issue is discussed further in Chapter 4, Managing Your Own Concerns.)

Beyond providing a glossary and doing some context setting, you may be tempted to rewrite in a substantive way parts of the story line or some of the characters. I urge you not to do that. Part of the power of cases is that they invite participants to enter into a story that is both familiar and new. Making the entire story familiar can make it difficult for participants to focus on the critical issues. Often, the very pieces of the case that are new or unusual are the pieces that offer participants some distance in order to take a critical look at the issues. If the case is too much like one's own situation, it is too tempting to focus only on the obstacles or the constraints that make the situation problematic in the first place. Discussion of a situation that is "just like mine" is hard to distinguish from talking about "me and what I do," and it is difficult for participants not to take personally suggestions or comments raised in discussion. Therefore, try to keep your translation work to a minimum. Let the discussion fill in the gaps of the case, rather than trying to translate or rewrite the case to spell out all the ideas or issues you want to see emerge in the case discussion.

At the same time, your work as a facilitator is to know your audience—the participants—and that knowledge may lead you to adapt some piece of the case in order to make it more accessible to participants. A particular action or aspect of a character or even a character's name may trigger associations or issues for participants that you would prefer not to have as part of the case discussion. As I prepared to use a case with a particular group, I found that the name of the central fictional character was identical to the name of someone in the district. Such a name would evoke the image of a person that I didn't want people to bring to the discussion, so changing the name of that character was a good course of action. (From a practical standpoint, you may not be able to make changes easily on the page of a published case. Keep this in mind as you select a case.)

With another case that focused in part on collegial professional development, there was limited information in the text about teachers' prior efforts to work collegially. The particular group of participants using the case placed a high value on collegial professional work and had devoted a lot of time and energy to it. I needed to understand what the group wanted to know about the characters' past collegial experiences, and why that information was important to them. In the ensuing discussion, I heard participants articulate different sets of assumptions they brought to the case depending on the level of collegiality they perceived among the characters. The case discussion was richer because the participants voiced their assumptions about collegiality. This richness would not have been achieved if I had merely specified more details about the characters' prior collegial experiences.

When I used "Oliver's Experiment" with the high school department chairs and administrators, it was helpful to define terms that were familiar to the mathematics department chair (for example, NCTM *Standards*) but less familiar to others in the group. Given that the participants were mostly department chairs, it was useful to hear how they filled in more of the context about how departments might operate (for example, extrapolating from the text that Bill, the department chair, was sharing ideas about assessment from other departments as well as from the mathematics education field).

My point is that the kind of translation I am suggesting is limited and purposeful. Before doing any translating of the text, articulate for yourself your assumptions about why something in the case needs to be changed. Consider how such a modification or adaptation might work for the participants. Then, make a note to see how it plays out during the case experience. How does it circumvent the problems you had anticipated?

STRUCTURING THE CASE EXPERIENCE

Once you've done advance planning, turn next to structuring the case experience. As I've mentioned earlier, facilitating the case is a recursive process. In this section, I focus on the second bend in the spiral (see Figure 2.3). I look at how to construct a "lesson plan," considering what the beginning, middle, and end of the case experience might be. I have purposely chosen to use the term *case experience* because what gets created among you and the participants is a particular experience, informed by what you know of this group, your goals, and the case itself. If you were to use the case again, even with a similar group, the experience of the case would be different. There are too many variables that go into a particular case experience to believe that it can be replicated time and again. What you, as the facilitator, can do is bring some structure to the case experience by the choice and sequencing of discussion questions and activities.

If available, the notes that accompany most published cases (such as the facilitator's guide for "Oliver's Experiment") will be very useful here. The purpose of these kinds of case notes is to offer a structure for the case experience through a set of questions and activities that you *might* use. For example, it is unlikely that you or the participants would have time to do all the activities or discuss all the questions offered in the facilitator's guide for "Oliver's Experiment." Therefore, even when notes are available, you need to make some decisions about how to structure the case experience for participants. There are at lease three tasks to consider when structuring the case experience:

- Identify an entry point into the case, the portion of the text that will most likely engage participants.
- Construct a sequence for the case experience.
- Use the available time.

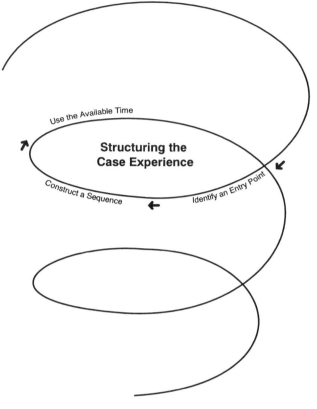

FIGURE 2.3

Identify an Entry Point

An entry point is the scene, character, or action that participants find most engaging or memorable in the case. As the facilitator, you try to anticipate what that entry point will be and use that information in structuring the case experience. The entry point into the case can become the portion of the text that you and participants work with most extensively, or the "hook" that galvanizes conversation, or the point of departure for a larger discussion. Essentially, the entry point is the portion of the text that offers participants the best opportunity to address the articulated goal. A powerful case experience makes use of the portion of text that participants find most engaging.

It is also your responsibility, as facilitator, to bridge any gaps that exist between the entry point that participants choose for themselves and the one that you might choose for them. In a complex and well-written case, there will be a number of possible entry points into a case. This is why it is important both to know the participants and their interests, and to know the case and what it offers, so that you can make an educated guess as to what part of the case text is an attractive entry point for participants. While this may differ from where you yourself connect to it, you cannot influence others if you do not at least have an understanding of where they would enter the text.

Finding the entry point into a case can be illustrated from my use of "Oliver's Experiment" with the group of department chairs and administrators. Recall that members of this group were in the process of looking at the issue of alternative assessment and were interested in thinking about its implications across the entire school. The questions they initially brought to this case were about the implications of changing assessment practices and the challenge of implementing such assessments in their school and community. I suspected the entry point that they would be drawn to would be Oliver's interaction with Mrs. Ramirez in the first scene.

My goal in using the case with them was to create space for them to learn more about alternative assessment and to test their assumptions and understanding with one another. I was therefore more drawn to an entry point such as a focus on Oliver himself, as an educator changing his assessment practices and figuring out the ramifications of his actions. By putting the emphasis on Oliver, I thought that we could pursue the alternative assessment issue more directly because we could consider what Oliver did differently regarding assessment and look at the ramifications of his actions for his classroom, and for other classrooms and departments. In this way we could get at the underlying issues about change. Other scenes, such as the one between Oliver and Mrs. Ramirez, would provide information, but that would not be the primary focus.

I had reason to believe that the interaction between Oliver and Mrs. Ramirez would be a less successful entry point for this group. Although many of the ideas that Oliver is exploring in his classroom practice are represented in that interaction, as the initial point of entry into the case for this group, this interaction would be limiting. It is difficult to move from the Oliver/Mrs. Ramirez interaction to pick up the threads of the process of change issue. From the perspective of a parent, any experience of a change process on the part of a teacher can be interpreted as "experimenting with my child." This is a critical perspective, but it is a tough one to focus on initially in the case when the group's goal is to explore the idea of alternative assessment.

Construct a Sequence

At the center of your work to structure the case experience is considering how you want to sequence it. Cases are typically perceived as realistic accounts of experience, as concrete and tangible situations. My experience in using cases shows that it is best to begin with the concrete—with the information from the case itself—and then move beyond the case either to consider larger issues that the case addresses or to consider how the case relates to participants' situations. Figure 2.4 shows this progression.

My purpose in this section is to describe this sequence of moving from the concrete details of the case to the interpretations and perspectives that lie outside the case text, and to point out the benefits of structuring the case experience in this way. Typically, when we think of using cases, we think of discussion. This sequence offers a framework for the different kinds of discussion you can have with the group, beginning with discussion focused on the case text itself, moving to discussion that begins to expand upon the case and draw on the narrative to consider issues not explicitly spelled out in the case, and then shifting to discussion that moves well beyond the actual case. The next

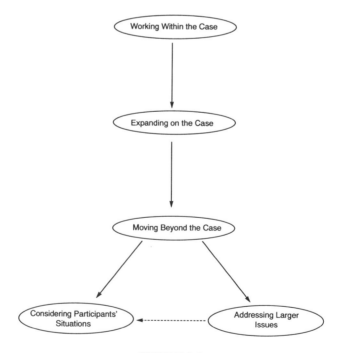

FIGURE 2.4

main section, Making Strategic Decisions, includes a more detailed description of activities that can be used for each step of the sequence, activities that are described only partially here.

Working Within the Case. Begin by working within the confines of the case, with the information, characters, and actions provided in the case text. As noted in the facilitator's guide to "Oliver's Experiment," there are a couple of different ways in which the case experience can begin. One is by describing the situation and the problem posed in the case, a strategy designed to get the lay of the particular land described in the case. Then explore contributing factors that influence the various characters and shape their options and choices. This part of the sequence is meant to familiarize participants with the case and its issues, and to begin to sort out the different perspectives that participants bring to the case from their own experiences. Focusing on the case itself, and the information provided or narrowly inferred, means keeping the discussion grounded in the concrete reality of the case. This is a good beginning for the case experience, since it utilizes the information that is accessible to everyone in the group: the case text.

When facilitating "Oliver's Experiment" with the high school department chairs and administrators, I chose to begin by posing the question, "What is this a case of?" to elicit the different perspectives that participants bring to the case. I wanted to work within the case and take the opportunity at the outset to get participants to articulate what they understood as significant in the case. This activity was followed by small group discussion that focused on articulating a particular problem in the case, a different opportunity to get the group grounded in the particularities of this case.

You also have the opportunity, early in the case experience, to utilize the portion of the text that you believe is the best entry point into the case for a particular group, given the articulated goals. As I facilitated "Oliver's Experiment" with a different group, I designed an opening activity that called for close analysis of Oliver's attempts to change his practice and the ways in which he interacted with Lucy and Bill in support of those changes. I asked participants to draw upon the information and perspectives provided in the case text, inviting them to work within the case in order to make progress on the goal that we had agreed on for the case experience.

Expanding on the Case. Expanding on the case means extending the discussion of the case beyond the text itself, so that participants can try out ideas or dig more deeply into a particular issue. Participants are working with the information provided by the case, but you are helping them to extract the issues inherent in the narrative or to consider how the action of the case might continue beyond the case narrative. For example, with "Oliver's Experiment," a useful way to expand upon the case is to articulate the next steps that Oliver or other characters might take, given participants' understanding of the important issues. This extends the action of the case beyond the final scene, using the characters and context of the case to, in effect, construct new text for the case.

This step in the case experience sequence helps participants consider issues or actions that are only hinted at or implied by the case, and to use the details of the case to frame their ideas. Think of this step in the sequence as helping participants to keep one foot firmly planted in the concrete reality of the case and to move the other foot into the issues that surround the case.

Moving Beyond the Case. The next step in the sequence is to move beyond the case altogether, either to address the larger issues portrayed in the case or to consider participants' situations in light of issues in the case. The choice to address larger issues or to focus on generalizing from the case to participants' situations depends on the goals for the case experience. As shown in Figure 2.4, it is also possible to move from a discussion of the larger issues to applying those insights to participants' situations.

Let's look at the facilitator's guide to "Oliver's Experiment" to illustrate this step of the sequence. The section labeled Looking at the Bigger Picture offers a variety of prompts for discussion to focus participants' attention on different aspects of the process of change, such as the pace and scope of classroom change; powerful reasons for change by a teacher, school, or system; and support for and barriers to change. The inquiry into these issues is framed by the specifics of the case itself. For example, understanding support for and barriers to change begins with consideration of Oliver and the support he had as well as the obstacles he faced. From there, the larger discussion moves to the kind of support that most teachers, not just Oliver, need in order to change their practice.

Participants can then consider their own situations, applying the insights gained from the work done on the case to date (including the discussion of larger issues) to the particulars of their classrooms, schools, or work environments. While participants will bring to the discussion of issues their own experiences, which may range far beyond the given situation and may even be entirely at variance with that situation, by beginning with the concrete case you can continue to anchor what would otherwise be a free-floating discussion of the issues. Spending the time and energy to discuss and understand the characters and actions of the case, and therefore the issues the case raises, opens up more opportunities to apply ideas from the case to participants' situations. Participants can look at ways in which events in the case are like or unlike their own situations, and at how the next steps suggested for Oliver would apply to them, so that the case serves as a shared vantage point from which participants can look at and analyze their own situations.

The whole idea of sequencing a case experience assumes the usefulness of planning the case discussion in advance and of clarifying the directions in which you hope the case discussion will move. This is another chance for you to exercise your best judgment as a facilitator in putting together a sequence for the case experience that will best serve the group and the goals you are hoping to achieve. Of course, participants' ideas and interests don't always map on to your intended sequence. You cannot expect to put together a sequence that will meet everyone's needs.

However, becoming aware that there is and needs to be a pedagogically sensible sequence to the case experience is important. It allows you, as the facilitator, to be more flexible in responding to the participants in a given situation. This may seem counterintuitive, yet your capacity to adapt to participants' ideas is enhanced when you have a clear sequence in mind and are clear about your goals. You can choose to set aside part of a sequence in favor of a new activity because you have an understanding of what you are trying to accomplish. Although the most powerful group interactions and discussions often don't appear to be highly choreographed, underlying those experiences is a logic or sense to how activities, questions, and events are sequenced. That is what you are looking for as you consider how to sequence the case experience.

Use the Available Time

Typically, we approach the case experience seeing the available time as fixed: "I only have two hours with this group of people. What can I do in that time?" As a facilitator, you may not be able to negotiate for more time with participants or secure quality time when participants have the most energy, although these are always options to explore. Aside from the actual time for the case experience, think about what time is available before or after the appointed time for working with the case.

There is work that you, as the facilitator, need to do prior to the meeting, as discussed in the section Doing Advance Planning. But you are not necessarily the only one doing some work in advance of the case experience. You can also think about what kind of work you might want participants to do prior to the group's convening. Clearly, you can ask participants to read and reflect upon the case. This preparatory work, though, need not be limited to reading the case. You can ask participants to gather information about the issues raised in the case. For example, a useful preparatory activity for the high school colleagues thinking about alternative assessment would be for individuals to collect information about uses of alternative assessment at their school or in other schools. How have others approached this issue? Such information could be used as a way to expand on the case. Another preparatory activity would be for participants to reflect on their own experiences with the issue raised in the case. If the case refers to a particular task, such as a mathematics problem or a science investigation, a preparatory activity would be for participants to do the task themselves.

The case experience can also extend beyond the time scheduled for the group to meet. At the end of the time allotted for discussion and activities around the case, what is the work that individuals (or the whole group) might take on? What is the "homework" that grows out of the group meeting? For example, the department chairs and administrators were curious about how the members of their various departments would react to the issues raised in the case, and decided to engage their colleagues in analyzing the characters in the case as a way to highlight different perspectives toward changing assessment.

Depending on the goal for the case experience and the direction of the conversation, another group might make a commitment to try out a particular suggestion in each person's own situation. The "homework" might involve continued individual reflection or writing, or participation in on-line conversations, if feasible. It might mean small groups reconvening to continue the discussion. Or it might involve picking up the threads of the discussion in subsequent meetings, whether they are focused on cases or not. This is most effective when the facilitator and the group are explicit about what ideas need to be carried forward and are committed to making connections between conversations. Thinking about the case experience as something that can extend beyond the specific time allocated for participants to meet opens up new possibilities for how the case and its issues can live outside of the group conversation that occurs on a particular day in a particular place.

Nevertheless, as a facilitator, you will be faced with a limited period of time when the participants will convene to focus on the case. How will you structure two hours? four hours? more? less? Consider how the variables of time and number of participants interact. An hour devoted to even a moderately complex case with forty-five people is most likely an awareness-building experience. The contact with the issues will be either very circumscribed or very superficial. The amount of work that a large group can do in a short period of time is limited, and it is best to structure the case experience with those expectations in mind.

Spending two hours with a group of twenty-five people opens the possibility of more and varied groupings for conversation and the likelihood of engaging in more activities. Two hours, compared to one, means that participants have the chance both to get acquainted with the issues of the case and to think deeply and creatively about them. Depending on the length and complexity of the case, participants need a good hour for "working within the case," particularly if there is small group work. Remember that the power of cases comes from their capacity to elicit participants' own perspectives and experiences. This takes time, particularly since you want to go beyond mere sharing of perspectives by participants into some analysis of their ideas. With two hours, you can afford individuals the opportunity to bring their own experiences to bear on the case as well as listen to and reflect on others' ideas. The latter are not sacrificed to the former, as is more likely to happen with a more limited amount of time for discussion and reflection.

A case experience of more than two hours, even with a large group, opens up many possibilities in terms of what can be structured. I've worked with fifty people for four hours using "Oliver's Experiment" and learned that the critical factor is the amount of time available rather than the number of people. In a four-hour period, it is possible to move beyond the stage of awareness of the issues into more substantive discussion of characters, analysis of action, and activities exploring the application and extension of ideas. Depending on your goal for the case, you can make a good deal of progress with people in a longer amount of time, even with a large group. This may seem like stating the obvious—that with more time, you can accomplish more. You need to consider, therefore, what you want to accomplish in that extra time. You can build in more opportunities for reflection, for hearing different perspectives, for revising original assertions, or for constructing new ideas. You don't want merely to extend the same conversation. A longer period of time means that participants can move beyond their initial response to the case, evaluate their ideas, and expand, adapt, or confirm their understanding of the issues.

Given a choice between more time and fewer people, I would opt for more time. For example, a one-hour conversation with twenty-five people will have a different tone and make less progress than a two-hour discussion with fifty people. The key, however, is in how you, as the facilitator, structure that time. You want to encourage and support conversation, but you want that conversation to have some structure and direction, too.

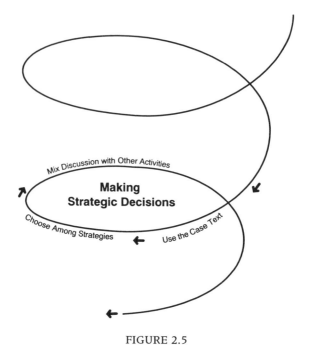

FIGURE 2.5

MAKING STRATEGIC DECISIONS

As with classroom teaching, there are strategic decisions you need to make about what you will actually do with participants. Various strategies can be used to achieve different ends. This section offers some ideas about how to do the following (see Figure 2.5):

- Use the case text effectively.
- Choose among strategies.
- Mix discussion with other activities.

There are a variety of tools you can use to facilitate the case experience, and this section provides a closer look at a number of those tools.

Use the Case Text

Reading the text is part of the whole case experience, so you will want to consider how you, as the facilitator, will use the case text. You can ask participants to read the case ahead of time; read ahead of time and respond to some questions; read the case when the group is assembled; or read parts of the case over the course of the case experience. Your task, as a facilitator, is to think about whether it is more powerful as well as pragmatic to have that reading occur prior to or during the time when the group is together. Either way, you need to consider what you want participants to get from their initial reading (or subsequent rereading) of the text. My decision as to when and how participants read the case text is guided by the goals I have for the case experience and determined by a number of factors:

- How much time do you have with the group? Can you afford the time for participants to read the case when they assemble as a group? How long will it take to read the case?

- Is it a good investment for people to use time together to read? Reading the case when the group is assembled ensures that everyone will read the case, even if it is a quick read. On the other hand, asking the participants to make a commitment ahead of time to read the case signals the importance of their work prior to the case experience and offers them the chance to reflect individually, particularly if you pose questions for them to consider.

- How much information from the case do you want participants to have access to at a given time? Particularly in long or complex cases, it can be useful to ask participants to read only a part of the text and, as part of the case experience, ask them to read subsequent parts of the case. In cases with a strong story line or scenes in which the action takes place at different points in time, it can be very effective to withhold part of the case text until participants have engaged in some initial discussion or activity.

The text of "Oliver's Experiment" can be used in many different ways. Often, I ask a group to read the case prior to coming together. I may ask the participants to note their general response to the case: What issues struck them? What seemed most critical to them in the case? Or I may ask the group to respond to the questions posed at the end of the case as a warm-up for the case experience with the whole group. Alternatively, I have distributed the case to participants when the group is assembled and have made the reading of the text part of the case experience. This can be a good strategy when you need to negotiate or clarify the purpose for using the case and want to frame the reading of the case text for the group. With the group of high school department chairs and administrators, when the purpose was to learn about alternative assessment, I found it useful to articulate this goal and ask the group to read with that frame in mind. Given the group's goal, asking them to reflect on the second question posed at the end of the text, What should Oliver do next? was not the most productive course of action after a first reading of the case. Instead, I asked them to think about how Oliver and others thought about alternative assessment. In another situation, with a group whose goals included problem solving, I might ask participants to generate as many ideas as they could in response to the question, What should Oliver do next?

I encourage participants to make notes or underline parts of the text as they read and reread the case, so making sure that each participant has a copy of the case is important. The text is a tool for the case experience, and the more carefully participants attend to the actions, characters, and story lines, and become aware of their reactions to the text, the more useful the case text will be in discussion or activities.

In addition to the initial careful reading of the text, you can ask participants to reread particular scenes or scan the text for information about a character. Participants often pick up details they didn't attend to in the first reading, or appreciate a new perspective when they reread the case after some discussion. You can invite participants to return to the text at points throughout the case experience as a way of reflecting more deeply on the case, taking a break from discussion, or seeking out additional information.

Choose Among Strategies

There are many options available to you, as a facilitator, as you sequence the case experience. The ones presented here are not a comprehensive list by any means. The strategies are grouped to correspond to the three-step sequence for the case experience described earlier: working within the case, expanding on the case, and moving beyond the case. Within each category, the strategies are not in any particular order and, as a facilitator, you will choose among strategies based on your goals for the case experience.

Working Within the Case. Typically, the case experience begins with a focus on the case itself. The following are strategies to help participants become familiar with the case and its characters, events, and issues. These strategies also help participants begin to become aware of and articulate their own perspectives on the case.

Getting the lay of the land. This refers to a variety of strategies that are good opening moves to trace the parameters of the case both on the pragmatic level (clarifying details about the case and its characters) and on the conceptual level (developing a common understanding of the central problem). Each participant will bring a slightly different interpretation to the case, and it is helpful at the outset to develop your understanding of the lay of the land. Determining the lay of the land usually happens through discussion questions ("What is the central problem posed in the case?" "What is this a case of?") but can also involve constructing a timeline ("Show the chronology of events, particularly the points at which Oliver talked with his colleagues at school about his classroom practice") or identifying entry points into the text ("Underline the part of the case that you found most engaging").

Analyzing characters. Focusing attention on the characters as multidimensional individuals, not unlike the participants themselves or their colleagues, is a useful strategy for developing a greater understanding of the characters' actions and motivations. A character like Oliver speaks and thinks from his particular perspective, which is legitimate and sensible to him, and analyzing him as a character is often a good way to help participants understand and articulate their own perspectives. Character analysis can be done in a number of ways. Each small group can choose or be assigned a character, with the task of charting out that character's actions over the course of the case, listing adjectives that describe the character, or describing the character's perspective on a given issue.

Identifying contributing factors. Compelling cases are filled with details that indicate the larger context that supports and informs the action of the case. Strategies that focus on these contributing factors can help participants develop a deeper understanding of the dilemma posed by the case or the issues that the characters are confronting. These can include attending to the interpersonal dynamics ("What is the nature of the relationship between Oliver and Bill?" "Characterize the interaction between Oliver and Mrs. Ramirez in the opening scene"), pertinent background data ("What is Oliver's past experience with changing his classroom practice?" "What is the climate in the district and state regarding alternative assessment?"), or available resources or systemwide concerns ("Which resources were available and used by Oliver?" "Which resources were available and not used?").

Analyzing actions. Part of the drama of cases comes from the actions that characters take, so analyzing those actions is a good strategy for pulling participants into a case discussion. Focus on an action that moves the story line along and is clearly connected to the goal that you and the group have articulated for the case experience. Action analysis can be done in various ways. Participants can list the steps over time that led to a particular action ("List the things that Oliver did that led up to his conversation with Lucy"), make inferences about a character's intentions at the time the action took place ("What was Oliver thinking when he began his conversation with Mrs. Ramirez?"), or construct a flow chart that displays the ramifications of a particular action ("Chart the various actions that Oliver took as a result of teaching the new unit Lucy provided").

Interpreting exhibits. Many cases provide information beyond the case text, in the form of exhibits. An exhibit is an artifact that is referred to in the case, such as a memo, a newspaper clipping, a chart, or a sample of student work. Interpreting or analyzing the exhibit provides participants the opportunity to bring their own interpretation to bear on the case information and to compare their perspectives with those of the characters. This can happen through discussion ("Does the memo convey the same sense of urgency about the situation that the character experienced?") or through activities ("Compose an editorial response to the newspaper clipping that described the task force's actions").

Completing tasks. Some cases, particularly those that are discipline-based or have their action in the classroom, include a task that the characters engage in doing, such as a mathematics problem, a science investigation, or a short story analysis. The task itself is a focus of attention in the case and generates some of the dramatic tension in it, so it is useful for participants to spend time during or before the case experience completing the task themselves. In this way, participants can compare their results with those of the characters and articulate their perspectives on the challenges posed by the task. They are then not solely dependent on the characters' experience of the task.

Expanding on the Case. The following strategies begin to move participants away from the case as it is written, and invite them to extend the action of the case beyond the text. These strategies keep the discussion or activities grounded in the actions or ideas of the characters but build upon the case to begin to explore issues that have importance or meaning beyond the particular case.

Articulating next steps. Considering what a character should do next in a case is perhaps the most familiar strategy that facilitators use during case discussions. Implicit in the ideas for next steps are participants' understanding of the dilemma that needs to be resolved; therefore this strategy is a good way to get participants to articulate their own perspectives. Generally, articulating next steps is posed as a discussion question regarding the central character ("What should Oliver do next?"), but it can be expanded to focus on other characters ("What should Bill do next?" "What should Lucy do next?"). It is useful to distinguish between short-term and long-term actions ("What should Oliver do in the next week?" versus "What should Oliver do in the next six months?"). In addition, you can analyze the next steps that the group generates in terms of how conservative or radical the responses seem and the underlying criteria for making that determination.

Replaying the situation. Participants can also expand on the case by replaying the situation. Imagine that the case text is a tape that you can rewind and edit what characters might have said or done at various points in the case. This strategy helps participants identify the particular interactions they find troubling or the steps (or missteps) that moved the action of the case in what they see as unproductive or problematic directions. Replaying the situation is also a useful way to practice skills, such as applying communication skills to difficult conversations or accessing resources that would have added useful information to the interchange. Role playing is a good way to help participants replay the situation ("Take the role of Oliver and replay his conversation with Bill, focusing more on the questions that Oliver wants Bill to think about with him") as is discussion ("What different response could Oliver have made to Mrs. Ramirez in the first scene?" "What questions might Oliver have posed to Lucy about her experiences experimenting with a new unit and new assessments?").

Revising aspects of the case. By revising important aspects of the case, participants have the chance to experiment with the implications of particular facts and contexts in order to speculate about the direction of the case under different circumstances. This strategy is useful in testing out the larger implications of a given issue. You might ask participants to assume that "Oliver's Experiment" was set in a small rural district rather than in a large urban district and reflect on how that new context might affect the shift toward alternative forms of assessment. Or participants might speculate about how this case would be different if there were no statewide tests or in the absence of NCTM *Standards*.

Moving Beyond the Case. The ultimate purpose of the case experience is not to stay within the confines of the case text but to move beyond it to consider closely the issues implicit in the case or to generalize from the case to participants' own situations. These strategies offer participants opportunities to utilize the insights gained from the earlier parts of the case experience and apply them beyond the text.

Framing the bigger picture. Framing the bigger picture means focusing on the major issues raised by the case, as articulated by you or the participants. This discussion may begin with how the issue plays out in the case but then move to a more general conversation ("What was the nature of the support that Oliver had to change his classroom assessment?" "What kinds of supports do you think most teachers need to embark on a similar change?"). You can situate the particular issue in a larger context ("What are the advantages and disadvantages of an outside force, like a state test, in changing assessment?"). You can also draw links between the issue at hand and other issues not represented in the case ("What are the implications for norm-referenced testing if more emphasis is placed, at the classroom level, on alternative forms of assessment?").

Connecting to the literature. Bringing in articles or even synopses of research studies or reports relevant to the issue at hand is another strategy for engaging discussion. You might offer a summary of some of the relevant literature and pose questions to explore the connections (or discontinuities) between the group's discussion and the findings from the literature. Or you might ask participants to read and analyze an article to consider its relevance to the issues in the case.

Acting as if "you are there". Inviting participants to enter into the case and explore what the situation would feel like for themselves is a strategy that can help them connect the case to their own experiences. A participant might try on the persona of a particular character ("Take the role of Oliver, experiencing the same kind of situation that he did, but act as yourself. Would *you* have done the same kind of experimenting in the classroom that Oliver did? What would *you* have said to Mrs. Ramirez?"). The purpose is not so much to revise the case as to explore what it feels like to be in a comparable situation and have to take action of some kind.

Springboarding. The case can also be used as a springboard, propelling the conversation from consideration of the case on its terms to reflection on the similarities or differences between the case and participants' own situations. This strategy might involve asking participants to describe the ways in which the context and characters of the case are similar to or different from their own situations as well as outline the next steps that they would take under similar circumstances. The earlier discussion of the case and its attendant issues can set the stage for applying those insights to participants' situations.

Mix Discussion with Other Activities

Working with a case, for most of us, is synonymous with discussion. Cases can lead to heated, reflective, or extended conversations. They can be a catalyst for participants to articulate ideas and get feedback from one another. Yet discussion is not the only avenue for exploring a case. A variety of activities can add interest to the case experience. Individual reflection and interactive exercises such as using images, role playing, and creating visuals call on different forms of expression and can lead to new insights.

In structuring the case experience, you are looking for ways to engage participants with one another using the case as a shared context. Some people do their best thinking and exploration in dialogue, others in some kind of hands-on activity. A successful case experience supports a variety of interactions. Similarly, some participants flourish in a large group, delighting in the give and take of ideas among many people. Others prefer the smaller, more intimate context of a small group, triad, or pairing with another person. Others need many opportunities for individual reflection. It is impossible to construct a case experience that will play to the strengths of every participant all the time. However, by carefully choosing different kinds of interactions in different combinations, you are likely to maximize the amount of time when most participants are fully engaged with the case.

In the next chapter, the section Incorporating Variety returns to many of the discussion strategies and other activities described here, but with a focus on how they can be used to facilitate the group so that a variety of perspectives can be heard and understood. Whatever mix of discussion and other activities you decide upon, you need to keep in mind your goals for the case. Selecting different strategies should help you and the participants achieve the goals identified for the case experience; it is not variety for variety's sake. Your challenge is to create a purposeful structure for the case experience.

CONCLUSION

The case experience both challenges participants' thinking and calls upon their feelings, memories, and hopes. This makes the task of structuring the case experience difficult but essential.

While you, as the facilitator, can start the discussion with a game plan, a structure for the case experience, you will quickly encounter the numerous options that participants offer for how the discussion might proceed. You are faced with the choice of how to respond to their ideas. You can incorporate their suggested pathways into your plan, trade parts of your plan for theirs, or stick with the original structure. As you weigh the comments of participants, their level of engagement, and the viability of the next activity or set of questions that you have planned, you need to attend to the bigger picture: your goals for this case discussion. If these have been articulated, negotiated, and affirmed in the beginning with participants, you have some anchor point for responding to the various options that participants offer. Improvisation is not only possible but desired, when you have a sense of the kind of "music" you and participants hope to create with a case discussion.

3

FACILITATING THE GROUP

Because cases are most productively used in a group setting, you, as the facilitator, have the role of facilitating group discussion and dynamics. Your charge in facilitating the group is to bring out, explore, and learn from the variety of perspectives that participants bring to the discussion. Each group is unique in terms of the experience, knowledge, and concerns its members bring to the case experience. There are, though, some useful approaches that are applicable to many different groups, which you can keep in mind as you work with participants to encourage them to articulate a variety of perspectives. These include getting the group started, orchestrating discussion, incorporating variety into the interactions, pacing the discussion, and achieving closure. The fact that you, as the facilitator, are responsible for these various tasks does not mean that you have to be the one to do them all. Nonetheless, you need to understand these responsibilities in order to take them on yourself or delegate them to a member of the group.

As in the previous chapter, I refer here to my own facilitation of "Oliver's Experiment" with a group of department chairs and administrators from one high school. My purpose in using the same example in this chapter is to highlight the decisions I made in facilitating this particular group. In addition, I describe some alternative decisions made in using this case with different groups to elicit and work with a variety of perspectives.

Because this chapter focuses on the characteristics of the groups engaging in case experiences, some additional background about this group of department chairs and administrators is relevant. These participants had worked together in the past and were not at all shy about speaking up and sharing ideas. In fact, I was assured ahead of time that talking was not a problem for them; finding enough air time for everyone to talk was more likely to be the challenge. The group had worked with other facilitators, including the building principal, who often acted in a facilitative capacity with this group. The case discussion was the morning agenda for the group, to be followed by another discussion in the afternoon that many members of the group felt was more urgent; thus there was the chance that some participants might be a bit distracted. Another potential source of distraction was the need that some of the administrators felt to be checking in with colleagues who were left in charge of the building for the day. In using this example here, I show how I factored this information into my decisions about facilitating "Oliver's Experiment" with this group.

GETTING STARTED

Getting a group started in a case discussion, whether it is an ongoing series of conversations with the same group or a single session, means that you as the facilitator have to answer some fundamental questions:

• Who are these people?
• How are we all going to work together?

The first question focuses your attention on the individuals in the group and the ways in which they are similar and different from one another. The second question focuses your attention on interactions within the group and norms for discussion. You will be much more successful in facilitating the group if you attend to both of these questions before you walk into the room.

Having a good understanding of who the assembled participants will be is key to good group facilitation. You do not have to know each of them personally or have a complete dossier on each participant. It is helpful, though, to have some basic information about the group. This is information you can try to gather before the group meets, so you can consider how it will influence your facilitation of the group as you try to bring out and understand the variety of perspectives present in the group.

Know the Group

Size. How many people will you be working with? As noted in the previous chapter, the size of the group has implications for what issues you frame and how you frame them. Similarly, the size of the group shapes how you work with the participants to elicit different perspectives. It is, of course, easier to facilitate a group of ten people than a group of fifty. This is common sense, but it also reflects the fact that it is easier to help ten people articulate their perspectives than it is to do that work with fifty people—and that is aside from the facilitative challenge of doing something with the larger variety of perspectives. As a facilitator, you engage in different kinds of work with different-sized groups. It is clearly not practical to bring the same expectations to working with a group of ten as to working with a group of fifty. Instead, you need to think about how you employ different strategies to elicit and understand a variety of perspectives in groups of varying sizes. Many of the strategies discussed here are applicable to both small and large groups. You need to be mindful, though, of how you employ them and to what end.

The group of high school department chairs and administrators with whom I used "Oliver's Experiment" had seventeen members. This size made it possible to have some large group conversation, although I have found that, with any group over ten, it is more productive to keep the large group discussions few in number and very focused. Quite often I used small groups, with four to five participants per group, which allowed for a lot of conversation.

Composition. What is the makeup of this group? Thinking about the composition of the group is a chance to consider how much diversity of perspectives you can anticipate in the case discussion. As I've suggested, case discussions are more productive and exciting with a variety of perspectives at play. If we all think alike on an issue, the discussion is only a reinforcement of our existing ideas and not the chance to probe, extend, challenge, or learn more deeply. Also, by becoming aware of the composition of the group, you can begin to think about the norms that will guide conversation: what gets said or not, who speaks and who listens.

When looking at the composition of the group, consider the following dimensions: experience, age, race/ethnicity, and gender. If you are new to case facilitation, this list may seem daunting. How, you may ask, can I possibly keep all of these in mind? Remember that it's helpful to learn about the composition of the group in advance and to consider what kind of impact it will have on the group conversation. Consider which of these dimensions may be most important to the group and to your facilitation of the group. Keep this dimension in mind as you observe and monitor the group interactions during the case experience. As you gain more experience as a case facilitator, it will be easier to attend to more of these dimensions.

Experience. What is the experience base that participants will draw from? Are they all classroom teachers, and if so, do they teach at different grade levels or in different kinds of schools? Are there district office staff, university faculty, or community members present? What you are trying to ascertain is the range of education experiences from which this particular group will draw. Having some picture in mind of the range of experiences, however preliminary, will help you facilitate the group more effectively. Knowing that elementary, middle school, and high school teachers are in the group means that you should make an effort to get those different perspectives into the conversation. In a cross-grades group, elementary teachers are often reluctant to participate in a discipline-specific case, believing that they do not have as much content knowledge as their counterparts in the higher grades. Knowing that university faculty and classroom teachers are in the group means that you should be aware of the kinds of language or images they each use to convey ideas. Many teachers find the language of university faculty to be more abstract and theoretical than what they would use to describe the same phenomenon, leading some teachers to withdraw from the discussion.

I was working with a group of high school department chairs who all taught in the same school, along with five program directors and three administrators from the same school, most of whom had been classroom teachers. I didn't know how long anyone had been in his or her current position but assumed that they were bringing relatively similar kinds of education experience to bear on the case and our discussion.

Age. What is the age range among participants? Consider whether they are veteran educators, novices, or individuals new to teaching but not to the world of work. Does their age correlate with the kinds of education experiences they bring to the group? What you are trying to attend to is the impact that an age range may have in the group. If the group is skewed to over sixty years or under twenty-five years, you should look and listen for the "outliers." For example, in a group of teachers with an average age of fifty-five and thirty years of experience, the two twenty-four-year-old teachers in the group may be less inclined to speak. Knowing that teachers with thirty years of experience and young teachers with substantially less experience are in the group means that you should take note of how all members of the group are participating and learning. A good case experience is one in which all members, regardless of age, can participate, not a situation in which some speak and the others only listen.

The great majority of participants who were using the "Oliver's Experiment" case were in their mid-forties through late fifties. There were no very young teachers in the group. Given this narrow age range, I tried to be aware of how the closeness in age might predispose them to talk about certain issues or avoid others.

Race/Ethnicity. What is the racial and ethnic mix in the group? Are the participants predominantly from one group? One issue to be concerned about is representation. If there is one African-American teacher in a group of twenty white teachers, she may be reluctant to raise concerns or points of view lest she be perceived as speaking "on behalf of" other African-Americans. Or she may feel compelled to speak up frequently to get those issues on the table. The point is not to argue for equal representation of different groups but to note that the racial and ethnic mix of the group affects the group dynamics and, as a facilitator, you need to become aware of and work with those dynamics. More important than group dynamics is the fact that, for many people, their racial and ethnic background informs their perspectives and beliefs in powerful ways. The conversation will be richer for the presence of these perspectives. Your responsibility as a facilitator is to invite and work with these different perspectives.

The participants that I was working with were all white and were teaching in a school that had only a small minority population. The issue of race, in terms of the makeup of the student population and the teaching faculty, was one that the school community discussed openly. As one member of the group commented to me wryly, "It's easy for us to talk about race, here, when it is such a homogeneous group."

Gender. What is the balance of men and women in the group? Consider whether there is a prevailing norm about what conversation is like in a group composed mostly of women or mostly of men, or that is evenly balanced. Aside from what the literature says about how men and women communicate differently, as a facilitator you need to be aware of the ways in which conversations proceed. Do some men (or women) dominate? Are there kinds of comments or ideas that are shared just by women (or men)? Again, this is useful information for you as a facilitator. You need to check your assumptions and those of the group about what kind of conversation to expect, and you need to develop an awareness of who is speaking and what is being said by whom.

The group of department chairs was relatively evenly balanced, with slightly more men than women in the group. Two of the three administrators were men, including the individual who was my point of contact with the group. I did not perceive any major differences in the quantity or quality of contributions by men or women but did note that the women tended to be somewhat more animated in small group discussion compared to large group discussion.

To sum up the significance of the composition of the group and its effect on your facilitation, focusing on who is in the group is a way to understand and manage interactions that occur among participants. It is also a way to build your awareness of often unspoken norms about what is appropriate to talk about in the group. Whether participants talk about the larger systemic context, that is, the policies and practices in place across a district, may be related to their age and years of experience in the district. A younger teacher may not appreciate that larger context; an older teacher may feel constrained by the context and not want to raise it as a concern. As the facilitator, you cannot possibly guess what is in people's heads and the decisions they make about what not to discuss. However, you can be alert to the ideas that are not coming out in the conversation that you would have expected to hear, and be prepared to raise them with the group. Considering whether the presence or absence of a particular issue is linked to the composition of the group offers you a way to think about and frame the conversation with the group.

Nature. Be clear about the nature of the group. Are they people who are gathered together expressly for the purpose of case work, have they worked together in the past, or might they continue to work together in the future? Obviously, people who have worked together prior to meeting for case discussion will bring knowledge of one another and share some experiences. Meeting with a high school English department to facilitate a case means entering into a preexisting group, with its own norms, to engage in case work that may need to operate under different norms. Working with a group of teachers drawn from across a district who may have a nodding acquaintance with one another means helping to establish some common expectations for the purpose of the case work and the ways in which discussion might proceed.

Some groups choose to meet together for case work, while others are less than voluntary in makeup. Knowing the reasons why the group has come together and how various members feel about being part of the group is useful information. Working with a group in which the majority did not choose to be part of a case discussion or have had limited experience with cases demands that you consider that participants may be thinking, What's in it for me? Often, talking about the utility of cases and the goals for the case experience can engage such participants. Beyond this, it is important to remember that some of the negative feelings you may pick up from some members are not directed at you but at their lack of choice about being in the group.

Cases on education issues are typically developed for use in teacher education or professional development of practicing teachers, or both. Having an understanding of how these different contexts affect the case discussion is important. A group of students in a teacher education program brings different concerns and experiences to a case discussion than do practicing teachers meeting for professional development.

All of these issues—size, composition, and nature of the group— have implications for how much energy or work you, as the facilitator, need to devote to helping the members of the group get to know one another. A small, homogeneous group whose members have worked together before may need little time for introductions or sharing of biographical or professional information. A larger, diverse group of people who have not worked together before may be overwhelmed by extended introductions and sharing of information. What is important is that people come to know one other, and how that happens or how quickly they develop that knowledge can be shaped by you, as the facilitator. Minimally they need to know one another's names. There may be other pertinent pieces of information that you or the group request, which will aid in the particular case discussion. With a group using "Oliver's Experiment" to explore alternative assessment, I might ask each participant to note one kind of assessment with which he or she has experimented in the past few years. Wearing name tags, using placecards with names, and spending a bit of time on any of a number of ice breaker activities are all options for helping group members get to know one another a bit better, in the service of a more productive case experience.

This discussion so far has addressed the first question relevant to getting the group started: Who are these people? Next, we have to consider, how are we all going to work together? What are the expectations and the ground rules for this group?

Work Together

Clarify Expectations. An important activity in getting started with a group using cases is to clarify expectations: What are the goals for the discussion? What is your role as the facilitator? How is the case experience structured? This conversation with the group should draw heavily on the work that you, as the facilitator, have done in preparing for the case discussion. As discussed in Chapter 2, you have to make a number of decisions with or on behalf of the group in order to have a game plan for your time with participants. Sharing this game plan with the group is a direct way to clarify your expectations about the case discussion and to help participants clarify theirs. You need to be receptive to their ideas and consider how they may be accommodated, but sharing your plan is not an open invitation to abandon the goals and structures you have developed in favor of something completely new.

As a first step, identify the goals for the case discussion. Talk about them briefly or write them on a transparency or on newsprint so that all can see. What is the purpose for the case discussion? How was it determined by you and/or members of the group? What do you hope to accomplish with participants in this or subsequent meetings? An effective strategy is to share with participants your thinking and work that went into defining these goals. For example, in facilitating "Oliver's Experiment" with the department chairs and administrators, I needed to articulate the goals for the case experience: to explore the idea of alternative assessment for the characters in the case and for the participants as department chairs, and to consider how teachers change their practice. I also needed to describe how I had learned that this goal was connected to work they were doing in their school to prepare to adopt new kinds of assessments in their departments and to coordinate that activity across the school. Naming the goals for the case discussion does not ensure that you and the group will meet those goals. Not naming them, however, makes it even more difficult to meet them.

In addition to identifying the goals for the case experience, be explicit with the group about your role as a facilitator. As noted previously, everyone carries a different image of what that role is, which leads to different expectations within any group about what a facilitator will, won't, should, or shouldn't do. You have an image of your role, and you need to share that with the group. This does not require a long and involved explanation, particularly if you are still trying to figure this role out for yourself. You do need, though, to talk about what participants can expect from you. Talk about how you will facilitate discussion (Will you be a participant? Will you share your own ideas?), how you will monitor the passing of time, and how you will help the group make the transition from one activity to another. If you have a particular facilitative need that you know you cannot and do not want to set aside, tell the group. If it is very important to you that the discussion end on time, say so. If movement around the room is distracting to you and, you suspect, to others, say so. You are a reasonable person, and you do not wish to constrain people's participation. Nonetheless, if there are certain behaviors that make you clench your teeth, it is better for you to inform the group and negotiate some ground rules (see next section). It is hard to think creatively or speak thoughtfully with clenched teeth.

Another part of getting started is to share with the group some of the planning you have done for this discussion and some of the ideas you have for follow-up. The planning you have done is an important aspect of your role as facilitator, and unless you talk about it, the group will be unaware of the thought and attention you have given to the case experience. Participants need to know that you, as the facilitator, have carefully considered what will contribute to a good case experience and that this is not a "seat of the pants" conversation. In this way, you invite them to take this discussion seriously, and you can turn more attention to the task of working with this particular group.

Talk about your plan for the case experience, since this is a tangible way to clarify expectations with the group. What are the various activities you have chosen or designed? How will they build on one another? You may decide that full disclosure is not necessary, since there may be a closing activity that will be more powerful if people do not know about it in advance. More often than not, the job of facilitating is easier if you share your agenda with the group.

It is a good idea to ask for the group's feedback on this agenda, but only if you really want that feedback. Be honest with yourself. How much tinkering with the agenda do you want to do? How much adaptation can you do on the spot? You can likely accommodate much more adaptation than you may think, and in the course of the discussion things will shift anyway. However, if you are confident that the agenda already reflects the needs, interests, and even input of the group, say so. Explain how you arrived at this particular agenda. Often requests for changes are a way of testing out underlying reasons for certain activities, that is, they are ways to share a perspective that is perhaps different from yours. For example, if someone suggests that all the discussions be with the large group rather than in smaller groups, as you had planned, check out why they want this change. Is it because of a desire to hear everyone's opinion? Can this desire be accommodated by other means? Can the views expressed in small groups be shared with the larger group? You want to be open to participants' ideas about how to shape the case experience. At the same time, participants need to know that you have a clear plan in mind. Do not sacrifice the one for the other. It is completely appropriate to request that the group trust your judgment on the agenda, especially if this is the first time you and the group have worked together. Just remember to leave time at the end of the discussion or in follow-up conversations to evaluate the success of the case experience that you have structured.

The amount of time you allot to clarifying expectations with the group depends in large part on the participants and their experience with cases, and on the amount and quality of preparation you did before the group assembled. Expectations can be clarified in a straightforward way in less than ten minutes, in order to check the assumptions that you have made based on the information you have gathered. You will need to take a bit longer if the group is unfamiliar with case work and is trying to figure out what the experience will be, or if you find that many participants have decidedly different ideas about what the goals or structure of the case experience should be.

This is a good investment at the beginning of your work with a group. If participants are not, from the outset, engaged in the case experience, it becomes increasingly difficult to draw them in or to manage their concerns as time goes on.

Establish Ground Rules. The kinds of ground rules you establish with the group are a product of your view of your role as a facilitator and the needs of the group. You are trying to create an environment in which participants can share their experiences and ideas and move beyond the stance "This is what I think and that's the way it is." Ground rules can make explicit the kinds of norms you seek for discussion.

The ground rules can be very basic:

- Arrive on time.
- Participate in the discussion.
- Be respectful of others' comments.

These rules are useful because they can build the kind of environment that supports deeper reflection and conversation. They translate into "Be attentive when others are talking and working," "Participate actively and share your ideas with others," and "Listen with an open mind to what others have to say."

In using "Oliver's Experiment" with the group of department chairs and administrators, I negotiated with them some very basic ground rules, like the ones just mentioned. Given that this was an established group whose members would be working together over the next year and the fact that this was my only interaction with them, these ground rules were sufficient.

The ground rules can be a bit more advanced and explicit, articulating norms for a somewhat higher standard of behavior and therefore even deeper reflection and conversation:

- Offer reasons or feelings behind a statement.
- Clarify or rephrase what you have heard others say.
- Build on the comments of others.

With these kinds of ground rules, participants are making a commitment to a more interactive discussion in which they will try to listen carefully and understand one another, not just air their own ideas. More advanced ground rules are particularly appropriate for groups beginning a large task that will call upon them to work closely together over time or for groups have difficulty moving beyond "This is what I think and that's the way it is".

Ground rules are really meant to make norms for interaction public. They are a way to test out the commitment of participants to the case experience. Cases succeed to the extent that participants put themselves into the activity. It is not up to you to make the case discussion a success. You can do many things as a facilitator to structure and support the case experience, but participants need to be committed, too. Ground rules can provide some structure for that commitment to be manifested.

There are two additional questions that are related to this discussion of ground rules that have implications for what you say and how you act as a facilitator: What if some individuals monopolize the conversation by talking a lot or focusing on a single issue? When is it appropriate to share your ideas in the discussion? As a facilitator, you hope that it is enough to have a ground rule like "Don't talk too much" or "Everyone, including the facilitator, shares ideas." Merely stating ground rules like these is not sufficient, however. You need to be more explicit about what you will do, as a facilitator, when faced with a monopolizer or given the opportunity to share your ideas.

For example, if you are concerned about possible monopolizers, say to the group, "As the facilitator, I may ask some people to join the conversation, if they have been quiet. And I may ask some people to save some of their comments if they have been talking a good deal." If you want to share your own ideas with the group, say, "I have ideas about this case, but I see my role as facilitator as making it possible for you to share and explore your ideas. I'll offer my ideas later in the conversation, and encourage you to think of them as another perspective (or an informed point of view or a debatable position)." In these situations, stating a ground rule is not enough. You have to anticipate how you will act, in your role as facilitator, to create an environment in which many people can contribute constructively. Your actions will make the biggest difference.

You may think that clarifying expectations and setting ground rules with the group is not necessary. You may think, "This is far too much work for just a two-hour meeting," or "I've known these people forever. I don't need to go through all of this effort." My response is that you do not need to have a protracted conversation about expectations and rules. It could simply be a few minutes of discussion accompanied by a piece of newsprint with a few ground rules. Also, it is sometimes even more important to do this work with people you know than with those you don't know because it is too easy to assume that everyone shares similar views when, often, they do not. In either situation, making a simple statement about expectations and negotiating a couple of ground rules may be sufficient. These actions are important in getting any group started because they signify the importance that you accord to the case discussion and to your success as a facilitator. They will pay off for you and the group in terms of richer and more productive case discussion, provided you all act in accord with them.

The following sections discuss various aspects of facilitating the group, illustrating how you can act in accord with the planning that you have done.

ORCHESTRATING DISCUSSION

Orchestrating discussion is what most people think of when they think of case facilitation. How do I get conversations started? How do I keep them going? How do I bring them to a close? It is important to consider how discussions are managed, but these questions are often indicative of an underlying mindset that, as the facilitator, you bear the sole responsibility for making good discussion happen. That is not true. You certainly have a role, but it is that of orchestrating discussion. Imagine yourself in the role of the conductor working with an orchestra. As such, you cannot possibly play all the instruments in the orchestra. The conductor depends on the musicians in the orchestra to play their parts of the music. You depend on the participants to actively contribute to the discussion, bringing their perspectives into the conversation. The orchestra looks to the conductor for guidance, for an interpretation of the music. The participants look to you for guidance, for your interpretation of this case as expressed by the structure you bring to the case experience.

So, it's time to play the music—to have the discussion—and you need to act as the conductor. As you orchestrate the discussion, there are some basic facilitative moves that you can make:

- Initiating
- Guiding
- Synthesizing

These facilitative moves are not just what you, as the facilitator, do at the beginning, middle, and end of the time with the group. You can use these moves throughout the case experience when you shift to a new activity or begin to explore a new issue.

Initiating

As I have mentioned, case discussions can be messy and complex and contain an element of the unknown—that is part of their power. However, those characteristics of case discussions make your job as a facilitator of conversation challenging. You need to manage conversation in a way that allows participants to be heard and understood by one another and build a conversation in response to one another's comments.

In initiating discussion, you strive to keep the conversation open. You want to invite different perspectives and try out different ways in which ideas build on or challenge one another. There are two primary ways in which you can initiate such a conversation. One is by inquiry. The other is by advocacy.

Inquiry. An inquiry approach is represented in the facilitator's guide for "Oliver's Experiment." These notes offer a variety of open-ended questions that are intended to get the discussion started. They are framed as genuine questions for which you do not already know the "right" answer and that you and participants actually care about. Beginning a case discussion with something as open-ended as "What is this a case of?" and encouraging participants to offer short phrases that capture for them the essence of the case is utilizing an inquiry approach. Asking participants to explore a particular character's perspective, given the available information, is utilizing an inquiry approach. You are inviting participants' ideas; they are not fishing for your ideas.

Initiating the discussion with an inquiry approach is a good way to elicit a variety of perspectives and to open up the conversation. Remember that, as the facilitator, you are trying to encourage participants to explore ideas and test out assumptions. Framing genuine, open-ended questions can help them do that.

It is important to note what an inquiry approach is not. Asking strictly factual questions that test recall of the case is not an inquiry approach. You may decide that it is important to establish a shared context by clarifying some basic information and to do so by querying participants directly ("Who is the teacher in this case and who is the department chair?" "Was Oliver trying out a new unit, some new kinds of assessment, or both?"). Just because you pose a question does not mean that you are utilizing an inquiry approach. But you can use information supplied by participants to inform an inquiry approach that opens up the discussion. For example, you might say, "Bertrand just characterized Oliver and Lucy as 'close enough colleagues' who talk about what they're doing in their classrooms and share curriculum. Given that relationship, what kind of support might Oliver expect from Lucy in the future?" What makes an inquiry approach is not the presence of a question but the presence of an open-ended question that invites reflection and elicits multiple perspectives.

Note that this work of initiating discussion is represented not only in what you say, in the moment, during the conversation. You can prepare some open-ended questions ahead of time and have them ready on newsprint, transparencies, or hand-outs. You can use the black- or whiteboard to record questions, script new ones, or assign questions to particular groups. While a good deal of inquiry happens in the moment, in response to ideas that participants raise as they are engaged in the case, you can also prepare in advance some thoughtful questions that invite different perspectives.

Advocacy. Discussions can also be initiated with advocacy. By advocacy I mean putting out an idea and inviting participants to challenge it, explore it, dispute it, or adapt it. The idea that you've asserted becomes the starting point of the conversation. Typically, we experience this approach as the provocative statement or the devil's advocate position, when a facilitator puts out a contentious idea about which everyone will have a position, usually a position opposed to the one put forth. These are powerful kinds of assertions, and they will generate conversation in a group. I have found that the advocacy approach works best when the idea you have asserted or a participant has asserted is one that is genuinely held. If you believe it, if it has meaning for you, you invite others to take it seriously as well. If it is unbelievable or outrageous, if it operates as a "straw man" put out only to be knocked down, it will elicit that level of response from participants.

For example, in initiating discussion about next steps that Oliver might take, you might assert that Oliver should continue to experiment in his classroom with different kinds of assessment because this is a powerful avenue of learning for him. You then invite response to your assertion. What do others think? How does your assertion compare to their ideas? This kind of assertion will initiate discussion because it is framed as a hypothesis with some specificity ("experiment in his classroom with different kinds of assessment") and because it offers a reason ("because this is a powerful avenue of learning for him"). A less successful assertion would be to state that Oliver should refrain from any future conversation with Mrs. Ramirez. It is not a hypothesis; it is only a statement of an opinion that is not very specific (refrain forever? until he is confident about how he is assessing students? until he has had a chance to think a bit more?) and offers no reason why this would be a good move for Oliver. It is certainly provocative and in this way will spark conversation. However, the discussion could too easily focus on what some participants might find outrageous or unbelievable in the assertion ("What school are you in that you can just ignore parents altogether?") rather than on the central issues that are in line with your goals for the case experience.

When you use an advocacy approach as a facilitator to initiate discussion, it is important to frame your statement to address central issues in the case experience. It is also critical to make a clear assertion without issuing a dictum. An assertion should spark conversation, not shut it off, so it is important to be aware of how an assertion is received by the group. If you make an assertion, does it get treated as the final word on the subject? Or is it a useful jumping-off point for the conversation because it acknowledges other supportable positions? Remember, your intention is to initiate discussion, so frame assertions that invite people to talk to one another. If you see that your assertions are having the opposite effect, refrain from making them. Or talk with the group about your intention to spark conversation rather than deliver an answer. Another strategy is to articulate more than one position that you or someone in the group might advocate, and invite consideration of a variety of ideas.

As with an inquiry approach, advocacy does not only take place in the heat of the discussion. You do not have to frame an assertion only in response to a comment or idea offered by a participant during the case experience. You can prepare some clear advocacy statements ahead of time and display them to the group in a variety of ways. Often, constructing a clear advocacy statement prior to the case discussion affords you the time to craft it carefully so that you put out an idea that really will open up conversation.

Guiding

In guiding or redirecting the discussion, you are trying to articulate, with participants, some emerging insights or important issues. Generally speaking, it is more useful to go deeper into a particular issue than to try to address the broadest possible range of issues related to the case. Digging deeper into a few ideas allows participants to stay focused and to make space for exposing and exploring their own reasoning. By digging deeper into a few ideas rather than collecting the broadest array of ideas, you can also avoid the impossible task of having to make coherent sense of disparate ideas. For example, if you initiate the discussion by asking participants to list and begin to discuss the various problems that they see in the case, you will quickly see that there are many possibilities. You can guide the discussion to focus on those problems most relevant to your goals for the case experience.

With the group of department chairs and administrators, the discussion began with responses to the question, What is this a case of? The group generated a wide range of descriptive phrases or titles for the case, which were recorded on newsprint. They ranged from "the troubled math teacher" to "what constitutes learning?" to "the uncoordinated department coordinator" to "the role of the standards" (that is, nationally or locally defined benchmarks for student learning). The participants' responses offered me my first opportunity to begin to guide the discussion by suggesting a focus on ideas that relate most closely to assessment. We talked a bit about the phrases recorded on newsprint, identifying the ones that, on the surface, were most directly tied to assessment. Building on this discussion, I then asked the group to consider a second question: What do you think the assessment problems are in this case? Even though this question was more explicitly focused on assessment, it still raised a variety of responses about the nature of the problem in the case:

- Lack of coordinated efforts across the department regarding new assessment

- Vague expectations regarding change and too many interpretations of what the standards mean

- "Walking the walk"—carrying out in your classroom what you say you value

- Fundamental mismatch between grades and new kinds of assessments of student learning

- Need for support (from colleagues and community) for teachers to change their practice

From this list you will see that there is still diversity among the participants' statements of the problem in the case. However, they are focused on assessment as a general framework. At this stage of the discussion, this focus is important and came about in large part because of the guidance I offered as a facilitator in framing questions and reminding participants of our goal. You cannot effectively discuss all the ideas that participants raise, so you must guide the discussion to focus on a few of the possibilities. You have to inquire more deeply into some comments.

The strategy I have described involved guiding the discussion by the way that I structured the case experience in my advance planning, sequencing particular questions to move the conversation in a particular direction. Other strategies for guiding discussion work more directly with the ideas that participants offer, in ways that focus the discussion and stay connected to what participants mean. These active listening strategies are described in the next section. They are tools for you, as the facilitator, to guide discussion to stay with participants' ideas.

Without access to these tools, facilitators will often guide the discussion by substituting their ideas for those of participants ("Thank you, Alma, Bertrand, and Charles for your good suggestions about what Oliver should do next. What we're going to talk about is a different idea"). Another pitfall to avoid in guiding discussion is the common pattern of serial comments, with each participant stating his or her perspective on a given issue. That pattern of discussion goes something like this: Alma offers her perspective, Bertrand offers his perspective, Charles offers his perspective. Alma restates her perspective, louder and more persuasively, Doreen jumps in with her perspective, Bertrand quickly offers his again, and Alma then seizes the floor to advocate for her position even more loudly and emphatically. Sound familiar? This common pattern of interaction is one that I think can be improved upon. Breaking this pattern means that participants need to listen more closely to one another and respond to what the other person has said, instead of reasserting their own perspectives. As the facilitator, you play a key role in helping participants break out of this pattern of serial statements and restatements and instead inquire more deeply into their ideas and the ideas of others.

Active listening strategies, while useful in case facilitation, are not limited in effectiveness to that arena. They are good communication skills, generally speaking, and are especially useful when it is important to respect and understand a variety of possibly conflicting perspectives on an issue. As such, they are good strategies to use in group discussions to guide the conversation to a deeper level. They are tools that you can use as you are talking with participants, to build on their comments. They are also strategies that you can use in written form by recording ideas on newsprint, transparencies, or the black- or whiteboard. There are three kinds of active listening strategies that you (and participants, too) can use to guide discussion: reflecting, questioning, and summarizing.

Reflecting. Reflecting is the skill of representing back to a speaker what you have understood him or her to say. This strategy offers several benefits in the context of a case discussion because you can

- Demonstrate respect for the speaker's statement by making an effort to understand his or her perspective, helping the participant to feel heard
- Check on the meaning of what you have heard
- Enable the speaker to clarify or add additional information to more fully represent his or her perspective
- Make it possible for other participants to hear the perspective of the speaker more clearly as you reflect it back to the group and the speaker confirms or clarifies
- Model for the group members the kind of listening you would like them to use with one another

In practice, reflecting can range from simply repeating what has been said, to paraphrasing the speaker's statement, to capturing the overall meaning or essence of the comment. Suppose a participant offers a statement about a character in the case, such as, "I think that Oliver shouldn't have said what he did about experimenting because it really upset Mrs. Ramirez." Reflecting responses could include, "You think Oliver shouldn't have said what he did about experimenting" (repeating); "Oliver should have kept his opinion about experimenting to himself, because it angered Mrs. Ramirez" (paraphrasing); or "You believe Oliver needlessly upset Mrs. Ramirez by sharing his ideas about experimenting without considering how she would hear them" (capturing the essence). The advantage to sticking close to the speaker's words is that you have a better chance of accurately capturing what he or she said. The advantage to offering a little more interpretation is that you have an opportunity to check out more of the meaning behind the statement. This is a judgment call for the facilitator.

Questioning. A second kind of active listening is questioning. This may seem counterintuitive, since most questions that we pose end up testing out our own ideas rather than inquiring more deeply into the ideas of another person. However, questioning can be a powerful active listening strategy when you frame questions in order to

- Help a participant clarify his or her perspective in order to advance his or her own learning
- Develop the group's (including your own) understanding of what that person is saying
- Promote a discussion that builds on earlier comments
- Model for the group members the kind of listening you would like them to use with one another

A facilitator can use this technique with an individual participant, directing a question to one person, or more broadly, directing a question to the entire group. Asking a follow-up question can be an effective way to help participants move beyond a statement that takes a particular position. When a participant comments, "Well, no wonder Oliver had problems with this unit—he never should have tried it in the first place!" you can ask, "Could you say more about why you think he shouldn't have tried it?" This kind of question can help both you and the group better understand this participant's perspective about when and how teachers try new materials, rather than simply understanding the speaker's position on Oliver's use of this particular unit.

There are a variety of question types that can be effective in a case discussion. These range from questions that stick closely to what has just been said and that tend to be primarily factual (such as questions that ask for clarification or for more information), to those that involve more interpretation by the facilitator and that are often more conceptual in nature (such as questions that pursue connections or invite generalizations).

Particularly in the early stages of the conversation, questions that stick closely to what has just been said are more useful than interpretive questions. Often, you can gain a better understanding of what someone has said by asking for clarification or more information, or inquiring about the assumptions behind a statement. Questions of this sort to the participant who said, "I think that Oliver shouldn't have said what he did about experimenting because it really upset Mrs. Ramirez," might include, "When you say 'upset Mrs. Ramirez,' what do you mean?" (asking for clarification); "What did Oliver say about experimenting?" (seeking more information); and "What kind of relationship do you think Oliver and Mrs. Ramirez had?" (checking assumptions).

As discussion moves along and the group has explored some ideas in depth, you can frame more interpretive questions that guide the discussion in certain ways. Such questions might include, "How does Oliver's discussion with Mrs. Ramirez about experimenting relate to his discussion with Bill about experimenting?" (pursuing connections) and "Are there other professional norms that Oliver is changing, besides experimenting in the classroom?" (inviting generalizations). Note that while these questions are more interpretive, they are neither very abstract nor evaluative ("Is changing classroom practice a good thing?"). Furthermore, these questions move the conversation away from what any one participant has said and invite the group to pull ideas together.

Whether you pose questions that stick closely to what participants offer or questions that are more interpretive, you need to frame genuine questions. It can be tempting to ask questions for which you already know the answer or for which there is only one obvious response. These kinds of leading questions have the opposite effect from the kind of active listening questions described here. With leading questions, you shut down discussion, since participants are likely to become impatient with being drawn down a certain path, preferring that you just tell them what you think. Framing questions that come from your genuine curiosity—about what participants think, how they react to one another's ideas, how they respond to your ideas—can keep the conversation alive. Moreover, these genuine questions can help you guide the discussion. Remember the orchestration metaphor. Questions can be tools for conducting the conversation (or music) rather than for putting words in participants' mouths (or playing their instruments).

Summarizing. A third active listening strategy is summarizing, by which you can accomplish the following in a case discussion:

- Offer participants the chance to hear their ideas in the context of others' ideas.

- Test out emerging meaning and offer a deeper level of understanding for the group.

- Model for group members the kind of listening you would like them to use with one another.

Periodic summarizing of the conversation can be useful for a group engaged in case discussion as a marker of how far the conversation has come, where it is now, and where it is going. It is another active listening tool that can help you orchestrate the discussion. It can be done in passing: "Okay, so far I'm hearing two perspectives. Alma believes that Oliver took a useful approach with Mrs. Ramirez, and Bertrand thinks that he made a tactical error." It can also be done more formally, to signal a change in the direction of the discussion: "We've been talking for a while about possible next steps that Oliver could take, and we've discussed five different options. Now I'd like us to try out these options by replaying the case. At what point would you have Oliver do something differently, given the next step you'd want him to take?"

As with reflecting and questioning, you can choose to stick very closely to participants' language in summarizing the conversation or you can be more interpretive. In restating what Alma and Bertrand said, you would be summarizing in a way that stayed close to their original words. If you wanted to summarize in a more interpretive way, which would go beyond their original words, you might say, "Alma and Bertrand are offering us two ends of the spectrum in terms of assumptions about communicating with parents."

Summarizing helps participants keep track of the conversation by reminding them of the key points in the discussion. It enables them to measure their own ideas against where the group is and track the different perspectives that are under discussion. By periodically offering a "bird's-eye view" of the conversation or inviting a participant to offer one, you can guide the discussion and keep it moving.

Synthesizing

Synthesizing is the third aspect of orchestrating discussion. Once you have initiated the conversation and used various active listening strategies to guide or redirect the conversation, you are ready to do some synthesis. You may be thinking, Wasn't the last section, on summarizing, talking about synthesis? Yes and no. Summarizing the discussion periodically is a useful strategy for guiding the conversation and giving participants the chance to take stock of the discussion. It is a tool that you can use throughout the case discussion to test meaning and begin to pull ideas together. Synthesizing is similar in that you are still testing meaning and pulling ideas together, but on a larger scale. Synthesizing needs to happen by the end of the case discussion, and it provides the opportunity to reflect on all the comments and insights participants have offered throughout the discussion, in order to draw out the big ideas, frame conclusions, or answer the question, What did we learn here? As a facilitator, it is important that you view synthesizing as a critical part of orchestrating conversation, and not as an optional activity.

Synthesis can serve different purposes, depending on your goals for the case experience. If you intend that the work on the case lead to a set of conclusions that have been carefully considered by the group, then your synthesis will be aimed at articulating those conclusions. If your goal is to draw out the big ideas implicit in the case that were aired in discussion, then your synthesis will need to highlight the insights offered or the ways in which the group constructed a shared understanding of, for example, the support for and barriers to changing a teacher's practice.

Synthesizing the conversation also signals that the case discussion is more than sharing a succession of ideas from different participants. It means working with those ideas to reach an understanding that is larger than the individual perspectives. What did we learn here? should not be reflected in the idea of a sole participant, as though one person entered the conversation with the right answer to the case. Rather, it should be a synthesis of ideas developed over the course of the discussion, in response to the stated goal for the case experience.

On a more practical note, you can shape the synthesis by offering your own take on the conclusions reached or deeper understanding achieved. Think of it as a first draft that you offer to the group for their consideration. You do not have to be brilliant and somehow craft the best possible synthesis of the conversation. You offer your best take, and invite participants to comment on it, expand upon it, or alter it. That is, the synthesis can be created with the group; you do not have to do it by yourself.

In using "Oliver's Experiment" with the group of department chairs and administrators, I commented toward the end of our time together that our discussion had covered a lot of territory—a phenomenon that is not unusual in case discussions—but stayed within the territory called assessment. I offered a synthesis of some of the ideas for the group's consideration, which provoked a spirited twenty-minute conversation. I

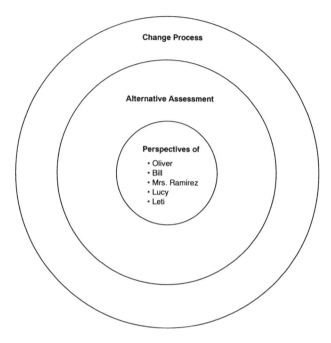

FIGURE 3.1

noted that we had talked about the perspectives of the individual characters on assessment and the challenges they faced. We had also considered
what we meant by assessment and looked at the underlying assumptions
about how change comes about in classrooms and across schools. I
sketched a set of concentric circles on newsprint to represent our discussion (see Figure 3.1), emphasizing how our thinking had grown.

Then I pointed out a couple of metaphors that participants had
used during the discussion to capture the nature of the challenge that
the characters faced as they used new forms of assessment: "the bottom falling out" and "religious conversion." Most of the participants
had been talking about the magnitude of the change involved with
new forms of assessment, and the unexpectedly large and different
challenges they posed for each character. It was not hyperbole to talk
about these kinds of changes as "the bottom falling out" of predictable
classroom practice or about these new kinds of assessment as requir-
ing adoption of a wholly new philosophy, not unlike a religious conversion. The conversation that this synthesis sparked was lively. Not
everyone agreed with the synthesis I offered, but many did. It provided
participants a chance to consider together what they had learned and

would be taking away from the discussion, and how their own thinking about assessment had been expanded.

Therefore, be sure that you let the ending point for the discussion be the synthesis rather than the bell signaling the end of a period or a hasty "Oops, we've run out of time, I'm sorry but we'll have to cut the conversation off here." It is very easy to neglect this step. As the facilitator, you need to take responsibility for ensuring that the group has the opportunity for synthesis. The conductor doesn't just stop a piece somewhere in the last movement because it's time for intermission. Instead, there must be some closure to the piece. It doesn't have to be a neat, tidy, or peaceful denouement to the music. It can be somewhat chaotic; it can contain some unresolved elements. It does, however, need to end in a way that enables participants to feel some satisfaction from completing the discussion, something more than turning the page and seeing that there is no more music written ("Oh, I guess we're done!").

INCORPORATING VARIETY

Using different formats can vary the group's experience of a case:

- Large group discussion
- Small group discussion
- Small group reports
- Individual reflection
- Visual and interactive exercises

As a facilitator, you are not seeking variety for variety's sake. Instead, you are looking for a combination of activities that will engage participants in different and productive ways. In addition to accommodating different ways that people learn, using a range of activities helps to get at different issues. A case experience that is all large group discussion, even for an hour, does not maximize the potential of the case in all its complexity and limits the range of perspectives that can be shared.

Figure 3.2 is the agenda I used in facilitating "Oliver's Experiment" with the group of department chairs and administrators. It is presented here to show how I structured the case experience to incorporate some variety.

Typically, we associate case work with group discussion. The opportunity to voice ideas and to hear other perspectives is a hallmark of the case experience. Beyond creating a time and space for participants to talk, think about the kind of structure you can offer to group discussion to make it a productive experience, one that pushes participants' thinking.

Overview — large group
    Articulate/explain goals
    Give overview of agenda
    Describe my role as facilitator
    Negotiate ground rules

Reading case — individually
    Read case
    Note response to question, What is this a case of?

Discussion — large group
    What is this a case of?

Discussion — small groups
    Frame the problem to focus on assessment
    Define the problem: What is the problem? Whose problem is it? What
       feelings are raised by the problem?

Small group reports — large group
    Share ideas from small groups, focusing on assessment

Reflective writing — individually
    "Write about your assumptions about alternative assessment that are
       confirmed or challenged by this case."

Discussion/activity — small groups
    Do character analysis, one character per group (discuss and post ideas
       on newsprint)
    "What is ____'s mindset about assessment?"
    "What is ____'s mindset about change?"

Small group reports — large group
    Share mindsets about characters
    Discuss similarities and differences among mindsets

Discussion — large group
    "What mindsets do you and your colleagues hold about assessment,
       and the changes needed to use alternative assessment?"

Discussion — small groups
    "What could Oliver do?"

Synthesis/wrap-up — large group
(Note: While I had intended to do a synthesis with the group, the actual form
of the synthesis was shaped by the content of the discussion.)
    Share concentric circle diagram (see Figure 3.1)
    Discuss prominent metaphors from discussion
    Talk about next steps for the group

FIGURE 3.2 *Agenda for "Oliver's Experiment"*

Large Group Discussion

Use a large group format when you want to create among the entire group, regardless of its size, a common understanding of the lay of the land in a case. Large group discussion can be used effectively at the beginning of the case experience to create a list of the issues in the case, clarify factual questions about the case, or make a first pass at characterizing the variety of perspectives that the group brings to the case experience. Large group discussion is also useful during the case experience when small groups report on their conversations, or as the group shifts from one activity to another. Summarizing along the way typically happens in a large group. Also, reconvening as a large group is critical at the end of the session to construct or critique a synthesis of the discussion, to consider next steps, and to end the meeting.

The value of a large group for discussion is that the participants all hear a common conversation and have access to a wider variety of perspectives than in small groups. Beyond that, the large group format can be used to build a shared understanding and to test out consensus about ideas. The disadvantages of the large group format, though, are obvious: more people means less "air time" for each person, and less time to talk or reflect can mean a more superficial inquiry into ideas raised by the case. For this reason, it is important to be strategic in your use of large group discussion.

I used large group discussion at five different points with the group of department chairs and administrators. At the outset, I provided an overview to the large group and talked with participants about the goals for the case. I also used large group discussion as a forum for participants to share their initial thoughts about the case after they had had an opportunity for individual reading and reflection. Small group reports, which are discussed in detail later, also happened in the large group. A large group discussion followed one of the small group reports, with the purpose of talking about mindsets that participants themselves have about assessment, in their own classrooms and school. Finally, we all talked about the synthesis that I offered the group. One reason that I relied on the large group format to this extent was that the group was relatively small (seventeen people).

Small Group Discussion

Small group discussion provides an excellent opportunity for in-depth discussion and analysis of a case. Small groups of two to eight people offer each participant more time to raise ideas, consider various perspectives, and sort through competing claims. In this way, small group discussion can support a more focused and concentrated conversation later, in the large group. Small group discussions also provide an opportunity to "divide up the work" of discussing the case and meeting the variety of interests in the group by having several conversations going on at once. For instance, in case discussions that employ character analysis as a discussion activity, each small group may take on a different character to analyze in depth and then meet with another small group or in the large group to report on their character.

The value of a small group discussion is not just in its size. For small group discussions to be effective, they must have some kind of structure that is apparent to everyone in the group. This may be a focus question that the group works to explore: "What are the factors that influence Oliver and his actions in this case?" It may be a specific task that the group is completing: "Analyze Bill as a change agent. What strategies are useful? What strategies are not?" It may be instructions about what the small group should be ready to share with the large group: "What could Oliver do next? Be ready to recommend to the large group two possible next steps, and give the reasons for your recommendations."

Few facilitators have the resources of additional staff to act as small group discussion leaders, so a clear structure for the small group discussion must stand in the stead of a person continually reminding the group of its mission. Even if you are so fortunate as to have discussion leaders for each small group, this kind of clarity about the task of the small group is important. What is more likely is that you are the sole facilitator working with three, four, five, or more small groups in a room. In this circumstance, you can circulate among the groups as they work. You want to be able to listen in to conversation, add ideas, and perhaps help to summarize the discussion. You do not want to have to deal repeatedly with the question, What are we supposed to do? Make the charge to the groups clear ahead of time by talking about it, posting it for all to see, or making copies of instructions for each group—anything to help each small group understand what it needs to accomplish, and therefore how participants can monitor their own progress. Explain to the participants what your role will be during the small group discussions, so they won't be surprised if you quietly listen in or if you join in the conversation.

I used small group discussion at three different points with the group of department chairs and administrators. The first time was to work on defining the problem. The second time was to do a character analysis and discuss mindsets about assessment and change. The final time was to consider what Oliver could do in the situation portrayed at the end of the case. There were four to five people in each small group, and participants stayed in the same small group for the entire meeting. Keeping the group membership the same meant that each successive small group discussion could build upon ideas raised earlier.

Small Group Reports

While commonly used as a tool in moving from small to large group discussion, reports from each group can be deadly dull. While the intent is honorable, namely, to share the insights developed in the small groups with others, the execution is generally boring ("Group #5, why don't you tell us what you talked about?"). A clear structure for the small group can rescue the reports from this stultifying fate. What you want to avoid is a verbatim account of what each group talked about. If it is important enough for the large group to hear the full replay, then all the participants should have been involved in the initial conversation. Instead, ask small groups to focus their reports to fit the charge they were given. That is, the small group can share with the larger group a particular aspect of the discussion, a summary of key points, a single response, a recommendation, or anything else that keeps the report focused and clear.

Reports from small groups to the large group are most effective when the reports complement one another, because the thinking of the groups is different, or because each group was working on a different dimension of the issue. If the small groups all have the same charge and are arriving at the same conclusions, then encourage the groups to frame their reports in ways that add new ideas to the mix, not repeat what other groups have said. Small group reports can be a kind of litmus test for the potential of small group conversations to contribute to a larger understanding among all participants. You want all participants in the large group to feel that they have learned something from other small groups that they could not have learned if they had stayed huddled together with their own circle of four or five colleagues.

In facilitating "Oliver's Experiment" with the department chairs and administrators, I used small group reports twice. The purpose of the first report was to hear and record statements of the problem in the case that focused on assessment. While I knew that each small group had discussed a variety of problems in the case, I asked that in their reports the groups focus on problems that specifically addressed the issue of assessment. With the second report, I wanted each group to describe the mindsets about assessment and change that they had identified with their particular character. Since each group had a different character to analyze, this report was more complete in order to compare mindsets from character to character.

Individual Reflection

Participants need the chance to reflect on the personal meaning the case has for them and their work. Appropriate prompts for reflective writing or thinking can help participants translate the lessons of the case into their own personal contexts. Reflective writing can be a precursor to discussion by allowing the individual the opportunity to reflect on his or her own thinking before considering that of others, or it can be a follow-up to discussion, giving participants a chance to respond to or integrate the ideas of others.

Study questions at the end of a case are useful prompts for reflection. Asking participants to free-write about the questions, ideas, or concerns they have at a given point is another good reflection strategy. (In free writing, participants write without pausing to reread or censor their thoughts.) Inviting participants to summarize the small or large group discussion can also be a good opportunity for individual reflection. Jotting down ideas about what to try in one's own practice or what to share with colleagues from the case discussion is still another kind of individual reflection.

Consider when to use individual reflection and for what purpose. It is a tool that is useful at many points throughout the case experience (prior to any discussion of the case, after large group conversation, as a bridge between small and large group discussion, or toward the end of the case experience to help participants take stock) and is a powerful complement to conversation. In my experience, the vast majority of participants appreciate the opportunity for quiet reflection and would be happy to write or think for a longer period of time than suggested. As educators, we do not have many chances to slow down and do this kind of thinking, and individual reflection on a case is often a welcome activity for participants.

With the department chairs and administrators, I offered two opportunities for individual reflection: at the beginning when participants read and reflected upon the case, and at the midpoint when participants wrote about their own assumptions about assessment that were confirmed or challenged by the case. This second opportunity for individual reflection was timely in that participants had just shared a large number of often conflicting ideas in the small group reports. At that juncture, individual reflection was a chance for participants to sort out what they had heard and consider their own ideas in light of the previous discussion. It also was a good stage-setting device for the small group character analysis that followed because they could draw on their individual reflections in this group activity.

Visual and Interactive Exercises

While there are various ways to structure discussions and creative ways to organize individual reflections, most facilitators and participants view the case experience as primarily text-based. You read a print case, you write some ideas, you talk through issues and report to others, and you see the ideas of the group recorded publicly. These are all important activities. However, cases also lend themselves to visual and interactive exercises that are not dependent on text in the same way and that can engage participants in different ways. Among these are imaging, role playing, and creating visuals.

Imaging. We usually rely on words to convey our understanding of ideas. We can, though, use strategies such as imaging to explore and communicate our ideas. Asking participants to create a sketch of a character that represents the salient concerns of that character is one such imaging activity: "Draw a caricature of Oliver that emphasizes the work that he is currently doing and the questions he has." A different kind of imaging calls upon participants to use their imagination to fill in the details of a scene that you have set through your verbal description. You can ask participants to imagine what the situation might look like if the group's recommendations were implemented: "Imagine what Oliver's school would look like in a year if he and Lucy made a commitment to talk to two other teachers about the kinds of changes they were making in their classrooms. Furnish the details for that scene a year into the future. What would be the conversation in the faculty room among these teachers? What would one of their classrooms look like?"

Role Playing. Cases are provocative, in part, because we all play out our own movie versions of a case in our minds. Asking participants to role-play particular characters in a scene can be a way to articulate underlying emotions that the text may not convey: "Take on the role of Oliver in his conversation with Mrs. Ramirez. Act it out in a dramatic fashion to convey Oliver's tone and body language." Doing a role play that extends the story line beyond the case calls upon even more creativity from participants: "Replay the case, taking the role of Oliver. You've gone to Bill *before* you've used the new unit to ask for suggestions about how to proceed. Act out the conversation."

Creating Visuals. Another interactive exercise is to charge a small group with creating a visual to represent a particular aspect of the case. Visuals are often useful tools for summarizing conversations or more deeply analyzing issues. Asking participants to create a concept map captures relations among ideas: "Create a concept map that shows the factors that influenced Oliver's behavior in the case. Indicate how (or whether) these factors are interrelated." (A concept map is a simple graphic that shows how elements are connected. In this example, the concept map might be a series of connected circles illustrating the interrelations among the factors that influenced Oliver's behavior.)

Drawing a flow chart of events, including possible next or alternative steps, invites participants to consider the impact of their suggestions: "Draw a flow chart of events, beginning with Lucy's initial conversation with Oliver, that represents how things might proceed if Oliver were to bring Bill into the picture earlier."

Visual and interactive exercises are a useful alternative to discussion in that they invite different kinds of creativity and often draw less vocal participants into the activity. They are good strategies for generating new ideas that then may be revisited in discussion. However, because they may be unfamiliar or viewed with skepticism by participants, such activities may be met with some initial resistance. Setting up these activities in a clear and explicit manner is therefore important. Remind participants that these activities offer a different way to explore ideas in the case, and are not intended as an evaluation of anyone's skill at drawing or acting. Encourage participants to try an activity, be ready to listen to individuals' expressions of discomfort or even incompetence, and acknowledge to the group that these exercises can be challenging for many. For participants who are skilled at talking about ideas, these kinds of exercises are a significant change of pace and call for new forms of expression. My experience using visual and interactive exercises with groups is that they are powerful strategies for bringing out new ideas to add to the case discussion and that even those participants who are initially resistant find value in the exercises once they try them.

With the group of department chairs and administrators, I had not planned to use any visual or interactive exercises. What I discovered, though, was that participants used visual images on their own. As each small group reported on their character analysis, I noticed that half the groups had created a visual representation of their character's mindsets, not just a list of phrases. This led to a brief discussion of how the remaining groups could construct a similar picture representing their characters.

PACING THE DISCUSSION

Another key factor in facilitating the group is finding the right pace. Spending too much time on any one issue can lose participants' interest; moving too quickly through the case can be confusing for them. You want to work within the plan that you have prepared, but you also want to take advantage of those moments when a conversation can catch on fire. Therefore, it is critical to monitor the available time and know when to move on to another issue or when to allow for more conversation. Here are some tips about

- Keeping time during the case experience
- The role of note taking in maintaining a good pace

Keeping Time

Facilitators' styles of managing time vary, but for most, time is a challenge. Either you tend not to focus on keeping track of time and are relaxed about letting conversation go on, or you are very aware of time and feel anxious when the conversation extends beyond the allotted time. Furthermore, you are working with participants who may have different expectations about how time is used. Following some basic rules regarding time keeping can be helpful:

- Respect the parameters of the session. Start and end on time. If participants want to continue discussion after the session, make arrangements for the discussion to continue, but stop the discussion at hand, allowing those who need to leave to do so.

- Give participants at the outset a general sense of the agenda and how much time you anticipate spending on various parts of the discussion. Planning the agenda (discussed in Chapter 2) is work you have already done, and it is helpful to share the agenda and your time estimates of the various activities with participants. Even if you are a very experienced facilitator, it is easy to underestimate the amount of time needed for small or large group discussions, so build in a cushion to accommodate the good chance that participants will need and want more time for discussion.

- Set time limits for particular activities and make them public. If you have said that small groups will have fifteen minutes for discussion, note when that time is up. Adding more time (or even using less time) is always an option, depending on the flow of the activity. But do not simply allow the time allotted to extend dramatically beyond what was announced. Instead, be direct with the group about how time is being used. Renegotiate with participants to add more time: "Two groups have asked for more time for this discussion. I'd like to honor that request by allotting ten more minutes for this discussion. Does anyone have any objections?" Or share with them your dilemma about how to use the remaining time: "We have half an hour left. I think we have time either to continue this conversation about Oliver's next steps or to replay the case—but not both—because I want us to reserve fifteen minutes for some synthesis at end. Which would you prefer?"

- Wear a watch or have easy access to a clock. Watches with timers
  are useful in this situation. If you find that you are not successful
  in keeping track of time during the discussion, you can delegate
  this responsibility to a participant. This person can cue you when
  time is up, or give you a five-minute warning, or whatever is useful to you. Articulate in advance what you would like the time-
  keeper to do and how he or she can signal you without cutting off
  conversation if the group is very engaged in discussion.

Time is a precious resource in a case discussion, and you want to use
it wisely. Therefore, coming into the case experience with an agenda is
helpful, as is being alert and responsive to questions or issues that participants raise that may cause you to modify the agenda. Remember that
your overall goal as facilitator is to support a rich and thoughtful conversation, not to dogmatically enforce time allotments on the agenda.

Note Taking

As a facilitator, you may take notes of the discussion for a variety of
purposes. I mention note taking here because I see it as a useful tool
for pacing the conversation. You can note ideas that you want to return to at a later point and thereby ensure a smoother flow to the conversation. You can make notes of ideas that are raised at the beginning
of the discussion and compare them to those at the end, creating some
continuity in the discussion. By taking notes you are constructing a
tool that will help you pace the discussion, since notes are a visual
record of the discussion for both you and participants that shows
where you have been and where you are headed. The following suggestions can help you to take the best advantage of note taking:

- Take notes on overhead transparencies, on a newsprint pad on an
  easel, or on a black- or whiteboard so that the notes are accessible
  to the whole group. Small groups can also take notes on newsprint
  or overhead transparencies, particularly if they want to use their
  notes in reporting back to the large group.

- Do not try to be a court stenographer and get a verbatim account
  of a participant's comments. It is more effective to summarize a
  comment or represent a particular point visually than to be comprehensive. Be sure to check with participants to see that you are
  accurately reflecting their ideas (rather than their exact words) in
  the notes.

- Be consistent in how you take notes. Do not write down comments from the first three people who offer ideas about the nature

of the assessment problem in "Oliver's Experiment" and then not represent anything from the next three participants who speak. For participants, seeing one's idea represented in the notes is an indication of its value. You might have run out of room on the newsprint and for that reason opted not to include someone's comment, but to that person such an omission is often interpreted as "I said the wrong thing." Be clear, therefore, about the criteria you are using in taking notes. If you are only adding new ideas to the notes and you hear a reiteration of an idea that is already in the notes, say this, so that the participant who offered the idea understands why his or her comment is not recorded (and has the opportunity to reframe the idea to bring out something new that you perhaps didn't hear). If you are recording ideas from all participants in order to go through the notes with the group later and look for similarities, be sure to inform the group. The point is to be explicit about the decisions you made about recording notes.

- Recruit an assistant or invite a participant to record for you if you have a hard time both facilitating the discussion and taking notes. For some facilitators, taking notes is a great opportunity to focus closely on what participants are saying. For others, it hampers their capacity to attend to participants.

- Consider the layout of the room. If you are going to take notes and keep them visible, you need to post them somewhere. Even overhead transparencies can be taped onto a piece of paper or newsprint if they need to remain accessible to the group. You might post notes on the wall in chronological order, or keep notes close to the easel or overhead projector because they contain key points you want to return to throughout the discussion. The notes become, in many ways, stage props that you try to use to best advantage in the case experience.

- Stay focused in your note taking. Your notes should help advance the case discussion, and therefore they should be connected to the activity or issue at hand. If participants offer ideas or comments that are not germane at the moment, note them in a different place. A colleague of mine labels a piece of newsprint or a section of the blackboard as the Parking Lot, and issues that are worthy of attention but not currently under consideration are "parked" on that list. This is an effective way to keep the conversation focused and yet let participants raise issues they think are important and have them recognized as such. For example, in discussing what steps Oliver should next take, one participant commented that many parents are being asked to change their perceptions of mathematics in radical ways. She was clear, in her comment, that changing parents' perceptions was not something she wanted Oliver to take up next, but it was for her an important comment that was noted in the Parking Lot. With modeling by you, participants can begin to use this strategy in categorizing their own comments ("I think this might be something for the Parking Lot"). If you use this technique, be sure to return to the Parking Lot list at the end of the conversation to see if the issues have been covered or if any of them still need to be addressed.

Note taking can be a good way to pace the case discussion. Not only do notes provide a visual record of the conversation, making it easier to connect ideas, but the action of taking notes can slow the discussion down enough so that everyone can focus on and understand a participant's or a small group's comment.

ACHIEVING CLOSURE

In facilitating the group, you need to think about how to bring closure to the case experience. This does not necessarily mean resolving the dilemma of the case to everyone's satisfaction, and it definitely does not mean determining the single best "solution" to the case. Instead, consider how you can end the case experience so that participants feel there is some endpoint to their work together.

Synthesizing the discussion, as discussed earlier, is a useful way to bring closure to the case experience. Returning to the goals for the case session and assessing the group's progress is another way to end the session. Deciding what the loose ends are in the discussion and distinguishing these from the ideas around which there is some agreement is a third alternative.

Another important dimension of achieving closure for the case experience is clarifying future plans. This can be on an individual level: "Now that we've worked on this case, what ideas or strategies will you bring back to your own work? How might you use insights from the case experience with the colleagues with whom you work? What support do you expect from your colleagues in *this* group?" If reflecting on individual next steps is not part of your agenda for the case experience, be sure at least to give participants a few minutes of reflection at the end to consider the implications of the case for their own work. While the case experience has the power to engage participants in intellectually stimulating discussion, it also has the potential to move them to take some kind of action. You do not want to overlook the latter for the sake of the former.

Besides considering future plans for individuals, you can focus attention on future plans related to the continued work of the group participating in the case discussion: "Now that we've worked on this case, what next steps do we want to take as a group about this issue? What issue do we want to explore next?" With the group of department chairs and administrators, it was clear from the outset that the discussion of "Oliver's Experiment" was one of a number of conversations and activities they would have about alternative assessment. Nonetheless, it was useful to conclude the session by asking participants what their next piece of work together would entail and how they would draw upon the case discussion. With other groups, it may be too ambitious to articulate a game plan for future work, but you can at least "take the temperature" of the group to test for continued interest in case discussions or other group activities, particularly if the group had only planned to meet to consider one case.

Last, but not least, consider what you need to do to find closure for the case experience for yourself. After the session, some facilitators like to review the notes taken during the case discussion and reflect on comments they and participants made. Others like to return to the original agenda for the case experience and compare it to what actually happened during the session. Still others choose to write a short memo summarizing the ideas generated by the group, for their own use or to share with participants. The point is, make the effort to find time and space to reflect on what you have learned from the case experience, both about the issues the case raised and the experience of facilitating the case. This kind of reflection can be a powerful way for you to find closure.

CONCLUSION

For many people, the act of facilitating a group discussion should appear effortless, lest the members of the group feel constrained or, even worse, manipulated in the conversation. This is a powerful mindset and one that I believe can choke off good discussion because it leads facilitators to believe that they should not play an active role in facilitating conversation. Good discussion comes through clear and purposeful facilitation, since it is an unusually perceptive and committed group that can engage in clear discussion without some help. To that end, I have described here the kinds of facilitative moves you can make to promote good discussion without constraining the participants in the group.

It is essential that you learn about the members of the group, since their respective experiences and personalities shape the discussion to a greater degree than the strategies that you may bring. Beyond that, consider carefully how to elicit the multiple perspectives that are inherent in any group of people and consciously work to inquire more deeply into the ideas that participants bring. It is easier—and safer—to work on the surface, with the apparent meaning of any individual's comment or idea. It is riskier—and more rewarding—to get beneath the surface and help others articulate some of the underlying issues. As the facilitator, you are trying to create out of the discussion something greater than the sum of the individual contributions. Be explicit with the group that you are working to achieve a synthesis, pulling together different ideas and testing their fit.

In facilitating the group, you do not have to be a solo act. While you bear more of the responsibility for developing and following a plan for working productively with the group, you can and should invite members of the group into this work with you. You are trying to engage everyone in the case experience, and there is a clear role for participants to play in this work. Remember the orchestra metaphor. As the conductor, you depend on the musicians to play their parts. In fact, without them there would be no music. Without the active engagement of the participants, there is no case discussion.

MANAGING YOUR
OWN CONCERNS

As you think about yourself in the role of case facilitator, certain dimensions of the role will seem easier to you, while others will seem more difficult. For some facilitators, working with and managing a group of people engaged in conversation and reflection is a challenging proposition; for others, it is something about which they feel confident. For some facilitators, structuring a case experience can feel a bit daunting, while others find it very compatible with their past experiences. Regardless of which aspects of case facilitation you find challenging or comfortable, I encourage you to take the opportunity to facilitate cases and to look upon it as a learning experience for yourself.

One way to help yourself in your role of facilitator is to become aware of and manage your own concerns. The model you carry with you in your head of what it means to be a facilitator shapes both the concerns you have about your role and the kind of experience participants will have with a case. From my own experience and working with other case facilitators, I have found that three concerns are quite common: the degree of control you wield as a facilitator, the extent to which you share or advocate your point of view, and the amount of knowledge you bring to the case. Each of these concerns is discussed in this chapter because by focusing on them you can begin to articulate your own model of facilitation. The ways in which you manage these concerns are as important as the skills you bring to facilitating the case or facilitating the group.

I invite you to think of case facilitation as analogous to teaching. There are many different models of teaching, which we can think of as being on a continuum. At one end is a very directive, teacher-centered model that offers clear structure and focus to classroom activity. At the other end is a very inductive, student-centered model that places a premium on inquiry and exploration in the classroom. Clearly, the role one adopts as a teacher depends on where one's teaching model falls along the continuum. The same analogy applies to case facilitation. There are many different models of case facilitation, also on a continuum from very directive to very inductive, from facilitator-centered to participant-centered. The role adopted by the facilitator is obviously shaped by the particular model one espouses.

I encourage you, as a facilitator, to be clear about the model you are using as you facilitate a case discussion. The discussion questions and activities offered in this book support an inductive, participant-centered case conversation, and the comments offered here about managing your concerns support a participant-centered model of facilitation. Yet I believe that it is quite possible and productive to use many of these questions and activities in a more directive case experience. The bottom line, though, is that it is your responsibility to be clear about the facilitation model you use, whatever it may be. (See Chapter 1 for a discussion of various models of facilitation.)

It can be challenging to understand and articulate the kind of facilitation you value and to adjust your practice to fit an espoused model. You likely will have at least an intuitive sense of the model of facilitation you are using before you begin to facilitate a particular case. However, most of us need some experience and feedback in order to articulate the model we are using and to align our facilitation practice with that model. Actually facilitating cases can help you understand the facilitation model you are using, provided you take the time to analyze what happened during a case experience. You can solicit feedback from others to understand your approach to facilitation, by asking someone to observe a case discussion you facilitate or to talk with you after the fact about the plans you made prior to the case experience and the decisions you made during the case experience. You can take this a step further and seek out someone who can coach you as you facilitate a case. Many people learn to facilitate by working closely with someone who has a bit more experience. Finally, do not overlook the help participants can give you in learning more about facilitation. Collect information from them during or at the end of a case experience about whichever aspects of facilitation you are curious about (anything from use of time in a particular activity to the plan you brought for the entire case experience). There is much to be learned about case facilitation through reading and reflecting; there is just as much to be learned through doing and analyzing.

BEING IN CONTROL

The facilitation model you use, consciously or unconsciously, is linked to your own concern about how much control you have in case conversations. This concern exists, to some degree, because there is an element of the unknown in case conversations. Some people think of this as the excitement of discovering new ideas, while others see it as the uncertainty of not being able to predict what will happen next. This is the nature of discussion with participants who may or may not know each other, who may or may not be familiar with issues raised by the case, and who may or may not have a personal response to characters or situations in the case. How you respond to these circumstances and the kind of control you feel you need to wield influence the way you facilitate.

It's important to think about the ways in which you do have some control in a case discussion. You can influence the discussion through your advance preparation. By developing a good understanding of the case—through reflection, conversation with others, and practice with its facilitation—and by structuring the case experience—through planning questions and activities—you can shape the case discussion. While you cannot predict exactly what will be said, you can wield considerable influence by creating an environment that encourages discussion along certain lines. As a facilitator, you are charged with articulating and being mindful of the big picture, the direction to the conversation. In this way, you can have considerable control.

You can also shape the conversation by soliciting the new ideas, the unique perspectives, the idiosyncratic experiences that participants bring to the case discussion and that provide you, and everyone else, with flashes of insight. These "aha!" moments are critical to a case discussion; they cause the conversation to have a liveliness and vitality that make for a rich learning experience. As the facilitator, you have the most control over whether or not such "aha!" moments are invited and supported.

Think of bread baking. For centuries, people depended on wild yeast spores to make bread rise. The wild yeast in a case discussion is the unscripted, often unpredictable, comments and insights that participants will offer. To the extent that you know your audience, you might predict what kind or amount of wild yeast is around. Is it San Francisco Bay sourdough yeast or some other regional variety? To recognize and depend upon wild yeast, you, as a facilitator, need to be open to ideas or comments that are different from your own, that stretch the boundaries of what you would expect, and that represent new ideas. You must be open to statements that "say it better than I could ever say it," those comments that are rich representations of ideas or interesting twists on familiar themes.

For example, in facilitating "Oliver's Experiment" with the group of high school department chairs and administrators, I saw the excitement that was generated among the participants as they did character analyses based on the actions described in the case. What people realized, as they reported their work to one another, was that they had identified very different issues as being critical to each of the central characters in the case. What Oliver cared about, what Bill was concerned about, what was critical to Mrs. Ramirez and to her daughter Leti were all distinct. This insight, this "aha!" experience, was not completely new to this group. They had all been classroom teachers, and such distinctive experiences were not foreign to them. What was exciting, though, was their realization at that moment of the extent of those differences and how easy it was not to take them into account. These differences in perspectives about assessment were apparent to them when they were pushed to articulate them, yet their shared perspective as department chairs and administrators tended to obscure the perspectives of classroom teachers, parents, and students.

I was able to capitalize on this unexpected moment by taking some time to analyze with participants both their excitement and the insight it offered them. One person noted that effective communication with a parent or a student depended on his ability to hold on to that insight about distinctive points of view. Another commented on how easy it was to pay little attention to other characters when absorbed in analyzing and understanding one character, just as it is easy for any one of us to lose sight of others' perspectives in our focus on our own point of view. I used these kinds of insights to set the stage for the next set of activities around mindsets about change, and to remind participants of them when it was time for us to strategize about next steps that Oliver could take in light of his interactions with the other characters. Could I have ensured that this group would arrive at these insights? Probably not. While I think that an activity like character analysis makes it easier for participants to experience distinct perspectives, I could not assume that *these* participants, with *this* activity, would arrive at *these* insights.

At the same time you, as the facilitator, can introduce some cultivated yeast into the mix. Consider how you can pose questions that act as catalysts in conversation. How can you get the conversation to rise? One strategy is to engage in discussion of issues that are contested or that touch on deeply held values. Another strategy is to seek out opportunities to push participants to look carefully at the assumptions and mindsets they bring to a case. Yet another strategy is to try to make connections among ideas that cause everyone to pause for a moment to consider the implications. As a facilitator, I do not want to depend solely on wild yeast for a lively discussion. I want to introduce some cultivated yeast to ensure that the conversation will indeed rise.

In the example of the department chairs and administrators, the cultivated yeast that I added to the mix was asking participants to reflect more deeply on the underlying assumptions that the characters in the case make about the changes necessary for alternative assessment. I did not want their understanding of the characters' different perspectives to be entirely serendipitous. I wanted to provide a structure that would either fortify their initial insights or provide a catalyst to prompt reflection on the characters' perspectives.

In evaluating the success of my own case facilitation, I try to ask whether I have been surprised by something or have found myself in the presence of a new idea. Do I, as a facilitator, have an "aha!" experience? What can I do to ensure that this happens? If I have facilitated a case a number of times or have become quite familiar with the case issues, I may not have that experience at the level of a completely fresh perspective or idea. I may have it in terms of the new interpretation someone brings to a character, or the ways in which parts of the case resonate with participants' personal experiences, or the connections drawn to issues and events outside the case, which cast the case in a new light. I find that when I try to look for such experiences for myself, and encourage participants to be looking for them, the case discussion takes on a different life. The stage is set by the expectations I bring to case facilitation: that through conversation with others I will arrive at an understanding that is different or richer or out of the ordinary, and certainly that something beyond the words of the case text will emerge. I may not know in advance or have control over what the new understandings will be, but I can influence the likelihood that the case discussion will lead to some kind of new insight for everyone involved.

I have learned through my own experience facilitating "Oliver's Experiment" that certain characters resonate more with particular groups than others. I had anticipated that this group of department chairs would be sensitive to the concerns and issues of Bill, the department chair in the case, and I was looking there for new insights about how a department chair deals with the challenge of alternative assessment. But by approaching the case experience open to learning myself, I was also open to evidence of new learning on the part of the participants as they explored and contrasted the challenges that each of the characters, not just Bill, faced in the case.

The opportunities for new learning and insight in the case, for participants and for me, outweighed the risks of not having complete control in the case discussion. We all know that the perception of having complete control is a mirage. It does not exist in reality, despite our mind's best attempts to make it so. Nonetheless, we each have different versions of that mirage that we continue to reach out for, like a thirsty person in the desert reaching for water. To reject that mirage of complete control of the discussion, I needed to trust that the planning I had put into the case experience, the choices I had made of activities to promote reflection, and my understanding of the group would support me to be open to the "aha!" moments.

SHARING YOUR POINT OF VIEW

It would be hard to imagine a case discussion in which you, as a facilitator, did not bring a particular point of view to the issues. You need to develop an awareness of that perspective and then act strategically about sharing it with participants. Often a facilitator is unaware of his or her own perspective on a particular issue. It is not that the facilitator has nothing to say, for example, about the kinds of changes inherent in adopting alternative kinds of assessment. It is just that she or he may never have had to articulate that perspective publicly. A useful strategy, then, is to reflect on your ideas about a particular issue ahead of time in your preparation for the case experience. In order to determine when and how you might share your point of view, you need to
• be able to articulate that perspective clearly.

Then the question shifts to what you choose to do with your opinion as you facilitate a case discussion. For what purpose do you share your point of view? As discussed earlier, your point of view shapes how you structure the case experience for others and how you moderate group conversation. However, as a facilitator, your point of view may carry more weight than you wish. It is natural for participants to look for solutions to the dilemmas posed by cases and to look to you to provide these solutions. What may feel to you like "just my considered ideas" may be heard by participants as "this is the way to think about this issue."

Does this perception of the facilitator's authority mean that it is not appropriate for you to join the conversation with your ideas, opinions, and experiences? Again, I invite you to think about what model of facilitation you want to utilize. You may have experience with, and prefer, the model of neutral facilitation, in which discussion ends and participants leave without a clear sense of where you stand on the issues because your attention has gone to helping elicit their ideas without sharing your own. By contrast, you may favor a more active style of facilitation, in which you join the conversation with the participants by articulating your own perspective. Or you may favor a devil's advocate kind of facilitation, in which you offer ideas that you may not even believe in, to which others can react. The extent to which you offer your own ideas is tied to how you see your role as a facilitator. Each of the models noted here has implications for the flow and tone of the discussion. Consider what kind of conversation you want to foster. Consider the facilitation role that you want to play. At a minimum, articulate to yourself and to participants your stance on sharing your own point of view on the issues.

In facilitating "Oliver's Experiment" with the group of department chairs and administrators, I gave careful thought to how I would share my point of view with participants. Our goal in the discussion was to learn more about alternative assessment and the challenges it posed for changing classroom practice. I had ideas to share about that subject, but I knew that everyone else in the group had ideas as well and that they would not be shy about sharing them. While I certainly tipped my hand about my perspective by virtue of the structure I brought to the case experience, it wasn't until the second round of small group reports, in the last half of the meeting, that I began to talk about some of my own ideas about alternative assessment and the mindsets that certain characters seemed to hold. Participants had raised many different points in the discussion, and I wanted to add mine to the mix. Then, in the subsequent activity where we focused on the next steps that Oliver could take, I took the opportunity to talk with others about some actions I thought Oliver might take that would deepen his and colleagues' understanding of alternative assessment. With this group, I did not feel the need to introduce my point of view early, as a catalyst for the discussion, since the participants generated many different ideas on their own. I did want my ideas out on the table for consideration, since I had a somewhat different point of view than many of the participants, so I made sure that I voiced my point of view during the discussion.

While I believe that there are several ways in which you, as a facilitator, can address the concern about voicing (or not) your own point of view, there is one model that I do not advocate. Using a case discussion to provide yourself with a bully pulpit is, in the long run, counterproductive. Cases designed for discussion are open-ended and inviting of different perspectives. If you, as a facilitator, indicate by the way you structure the case discussion, champion a particular idea, or steer conversation away from certain issues that there is only one appropriate point of view, you will effectively squelch discussion. Then the energy that you and participants put into reading, reflecting, discussing, and engaging in related activities is essentially wasted. There are easier and more effective forums than a case discussion to deliver a lecture expressing your views.

What you are looking for is a middle course between having the final word on a particular issue and having nothing to say to the group. Where that middle course lies says a good deal about how you perceive your authority in the group and the weight your ideas carry with the group. As a facilitator who has put time and energy into structuring the case experience and who has shown a real interest in the case, you will likely be seen as someone who has a stake in a particular point of view or a solution to the dilemma posed by the case. You need to manage such perceptions so that you have the opportunity to share your point of view in ways that contribute to the discussion.

SORTING OUT WHAT YOU KNOW AND DO NOT KNOW

As a facilitator, are you expected to be the expert on the issues raised in the case? Do participants expect this of you? Do you expect this of yourself? If case facilitation were synonymous with expertise, there would probably be very few people facilitating cases, particularly cases that take on challenging issues. Yet it is just those kinds of challenging cases that we need to understand, think deeply about, and discuss with others. Therefore, "knowing it all" should not be an expectation that you or participants hold for you as a facilitator.

While it is useful to consider what kinds of solutions you might offer to the dilemmas posed in the case, the quality or quantity of your solutions should not be the measure of your competence as a facilitator. Nor should the depth and breadth of your knowledge of the issues be an indicator of your success as a facilitator. Your knowledge about your role as a case facilitator, one who helps others engage in productive conversation, is distinct from your expertise on the case issues or your capacity to generate solutions. I would maintain that while you may be more comfortable in your facilitator role when you bring to it greater expertise on the issues, you may not necessarily do a better job helping others to engage with the case.

A similar argument can be made regarding what you know and do not know about the case itself. Cases designed for discussion are typically limited in length and scope. They cannot possibly provide all the information, context, or background one would want to fully understand the situation they depict. Yet, because the characters, settings, and dilemmas are usually so realistic and compelling, participants tend to become very curious about them and the larger context from which they are drawn. You will be tempted to satisfy their curiosity, but I would advise you not to feel that it is your responsibility as a facilitator to "fill in the blanks" by providing information about the case that participants want to know. Your ability to do so is probably limited anyway, but even if you knew all the background details, you could play a more helpful role by inquiring why a particular piece of information seems important.

In using "Oliver's Experiment" with different groups, for example, I have found that many people want to know more about Lucy, Oliver's colleague, and her background. Engaging participants in conversation about their curiosity, and why they want more information about Lucy, has proven helpful. Some participants speculate that Lucy is most likely a resource teacher in the school and that it is part of her job to work with colleagues in the way she worked with Oliver. Others characterize her as an "eager beaver," enthusiastic about her teaching but possibly not very skilled in sharing her ideas with others. Still others see Lucy as a "typical" teacher—one who happened to have some materials that a colleague like Oliver would find useful and was willing to share them. The reality is that I don't know any more about Lucy than what is included in the case text. The assumptions that various participants make about this character, though, offer a wonderful window into their own thinking about the role, experiences, and capacity of someone like Lucy and the ways she might work with a colleague. The conversation about everyone's assumptions about Lucy is much more revealing and contributes more to the case experience than would dispensing the "truth" about her, even if I had that information.

You can also discuss with the group what kinds of assumptions the group wants to make about a character or a situation, and take the opportunity to reflect together on why certain assumptions about motive, experience, or context are being made. You can use the absence of information in the case as a way to understand how participants read their own experiences into the case and how individuals use their own values and experiences as filters in making sense of the limited amount of information in the case.

With "Oliver's Experiment," the group of department chairs and administrators got into a spirited conversation about how Bill, the department chair in the case, was similar to and different from themselves. One participant interpreted Bill's interactions with Oliver this way: "Bill didn't really cut Oliver off. I'm sure he knew what Oliver was doing and was encouraging him to do what he felt most comfortable doing." What was behind this interpretation was the experience of the person speaking ("I would never leave someone hanging like that. I'm sure Bill and Oliver had talked about alternative assessment before, probably with the rest of the mathematics department"), which came out when I asked the participant to share his perception of Bill and Oliver's history. I did not want the conversation to focus on the inferences participants brought ("Obviously, Bill and Oliver have spoken before about alternative assessment." "What do you mean? It's clear that this was one more superficial conversation between two people in a department!"). I wanted our discussion to move beyond whether Bill and Oliver had spoken at length or not—a fact that we were inferring—and into an examination of the importance of Bill and Oliver's speaking together about alternative assessment and what the nature of such a discussion could be. I framed this part of the discussion as the chance to inquire more deeply into the kinds of thinking about alternative assessment that characters like these need to have rather than framing it as the chance for me to declare which inferences about Bill and Oliver should rule the day.

It is easy to perceive questions that extend beyond your knowledge—of the case or of the issues raised in the case—as a challenge to your competence as a facilitator ("If I were really prepared, I would know these things"). Instead, look at these queries as the chance to learn more about the participants' perspectives. Their questions, and the assumptions underlying them, are more valuable in the conversation than many of the "answers" you might be able to provide.

CONCLUSION

It is far more effective to develop an awareness of the concerns that you have around facilitating cases than to set them aside as feelings you somehow should not have. Your capacity to be an effective facilitator, one who can promote thoughtful discussion and utilize a case for maximum impact, depends on your awareness of the strengths you bring and the challenges you face as you engage in this work. In this chapter, I have discussed three of those pressing concerns: being in control, sharing your point of view, and sorting out what you know and do not know. You may have other concerns you face as you facilitate cases. The important thing is to develop your awareness of these concerns as things to which you should pay attention, consider how these concerns affect you as a facilitator, and look for ways in which others (participants or colleagues) can support you in addressing these concerns.

Throughout this book, I have articulated a framework for facilitating cases that places emphasis on being purposeful in the choices you make as you facilitate cases with different groups. As a result of reading and thinking about the ideas presented here, I hope that you have the growing capacity and commitment to facilitate group conversation in ways that open up issues and help participants develop a deeper understanding; to develop a structure for facilitating the case and to share that with participants; and to take the time and energy to reflect on your own concerns and interests in facilitating cases with others.

A P P E N D I X

OLIVER'S EXPERIMENT

In 1993 the Los Angeles Educational Partnership (LAEP), a public education fund, commissioned Education Development Center to develop two cases for its School-Wide Change Project within Los Angeles area schools. This initiative consisted of seminars and on-site assistance for teams of teachers, administrators, and parents committed to creating curriculum-based changes in their schools. The cases reflect the complexity and challenge of classroom change efforts, particularly the schoolwide implications of those changes. The cases were intended to offer users opportunities to reflect upon, discuss, and resolve critical reform issues.

"Oliver's Experiment" is about change from the perspective of an individual high school teacher as he works to bring his mathematics curriculum, instruction, and assessment in line with the National Council of Teachers of Mathematics' *Curriculum and Evaluation Standards* and other reform guidelines. The case also considers the teacher's relationships and communication with other individuals (a parent, a fellow teacher, and a department head) and looks at how their different perspectives, interests, and concerns can affect a teacher's attempt to change.

The characters and events described in "Oliver's Experiment" are fictional, although the case does represent real issues and challenges encountered by teachers in Los Angeles and elsewhere involved in schoolwide change efforts. The development of this case was funded by LAEP.

Characters

Oliver Wright, mathematics teacher at Grove High

Leti Ramirez, student in Oliver's geometry class

Jovita Ramirez, mother of Leti

Bill Chamberlain, mathematics department head at Grove High

Lucy Dobbs, mathematics teacher at Grove High

Glossary

California Mathematics Framework. Curriculum framework in mathematics for the state of California, describing what students should know and be able to do at various grade levels.

CLAS tests. California Learning Assessment System, open-ended problems and enhanced multiple-choice test items linked to the *California Mathematics Framework.*

NCTM *Standards.* Standards in mathematics for curriculum, instruction, and assessment developed by the National Council of Teachers of Mathematics.

Off-track. Time when various groups of teachers (and students) are on vacation at year-round schools

THE CASE

Nancy Cali, Barbara Miller, Ilene Kantrov, and Cynthia Lang

Oliver Wright held the classroom door for Jovita Ramirez, wondering what had moved her to come in for a personal conference. Parent involvement at Grove High School was still highly unusual, even though faculty members had recently intensified their efforts to increase it. He offered her a chair and sat across the table from her. Mrs. Ramirez cleared her throat, but then said nothing. Oliver tried to help her get started. "So, Mrs. Ramirez, you said over the phone you'd like to talk with me about Leti's math work?"

Mrs. Ramirez looked pained, but determined. "Yes, Mr. Wright, I did. I know it's only early November, and maybe Leti still has to get used to you, but I'm very worried. Leti was bringing home A and B tests last year. She liked math and was good at it. Last Friday, she brought home a test with a C on it." Mrs. Ramirez laid the test on the table between them. "Leti never gets C's in math."

Oliver smiled inwardly, Is this all? The Lake Wobegon effect strikes again—all parents want their kids to be above average. "I understand your concern, Mrs. Ramirez. But let me say that a C is not really a bad grade. In my class, a C means that a student can demonstrate her understanding of basic mathematical concepts and can use those concepts and her thinking skills to solve simple problems."

"But Leti says she *doesn't* understand. She doesn't know what you want from her. I don't really, either," Mrs. Ramirez continued, tapping her finger on the test. "They have to work with each other on one of these problems? Leti said she had to spend ten minutes just explaining this problem to the other students in her group. And you ask her here to *write* about how she solved the problem. And here, in question five, you tell her to solve the problem in *two different ways*? What is all of this for? Math wasn't like this when I went to school. Why can't you give her normal tests like the ones she had last year? She understood how to study for those. She did well on them."

As Oliver listened to Mrs. Ramirez's descriptions of the test, he realized how foreign it must look to the average person. He had to admit that it looked pretty different to him, too. Aloud, he explained to Mrs. Ramirez that he was trying to respond to research that had shown that "normal" multiple-choice tests didn't assess many of the important skills that students needed to learn and didn't allow them to use the range of skills that they brought to their understanding of mathematics. He told her about the NCTM *Standards*, California's CLAS tests, and the school's decision to examine its assessment practices.

Mrs. Ramirez didn't seem reassured. "If you don't give her regular tests, she won't pass the tests for college. She might not get a scholarship. She wants to go to college. *We* want her to go to college. She *has* to do well on those tests. And I'm afraid that you're not preparing her for them."

"I hope that that's not true, Mrs. Ramirez. I think that as Leti gets better at complex thinking skills and at communicating her thinking to others, she'll also improve her ability to do well on standardized tests." Oliver realized that he sounded as if he were trying to convince *himself*.

"I don't know. . . . Are all the tests going to be like this? Are these scores going to count towards Leti's grade?"

Oliver felt a momentary surge of panic. He didn't really *know* whether he was going to count this test's scores in figuring the students' grades. It was all so new to him. "Well, that's a good question. Sometimes, we assess students to find out how we're doing, so we can teach them better. I'm trying something new, and I hope I'm learning from it as much as the students are. As long as this new assessment is in its experimental stage, I'll certainly keep that in mind when grading the students."

"Well, Mr. Wright, I don't think you should be experimenting on my daughter. What if your experiments don't work? What if Leti doesn't get into college because she gets bad grades and low test scores because of your experiments?"

Oliver did his best to reassure Mrs. Ramirez that he wouldn't allow Leti to fall behind or get lost in math. They ended the meeting with an agreement that they would talk again after Leti's next test.

"I always said I wanted more parent participation," Oliver thought ruefully after Mrs. Ramirez left. "And now that I've got it I don't like it!" He felt depressed and troubled. He was perplexed by his reaction—he'd had a few really antagonistic meetings with parents, and they hadn't bothered him nearly as much as this one. Gradually, he realized that Mrs. Ramirez's visit had uncovered a lot of his own discomfort and uncertainty about what he was doing. He knew that getting feedback from others was important, but it was hard to hear his own doubts voiced by Mrs. Ramirez.

It was time to ask himself some important questions that he had avoided until now: What do I really believe? Are the changes I'm trying to make really worth all this trouble? What is it that I really want to accomplish, anyway?

Background

Bill Chamberlain, the mathematics department head, was one of the people who had influenced Oliver to try some changes in his assessment practices. In the abstract, Bill believed in the reforms advocated by NCTM and the *California Mathematics Framework*. They made sense to him, and it was clear that they were being widely accepted as the new direction for school mathematics. His own classroom practice, however, continued to be traditional more often than not.

Bill and the other department heads at Grove High School, after many discussions among themselves and with school administrators, had concluded last year that it was time to look at testing and assessment practices in the school in light of the state's CLAS tests and the current reform movements. As a result, Bill had sent a brief memo to Oliver and the other mathematics teachers in June, asking them to "think about the new ideas in assessment put forth in the *Standards* and the *California Framework*" and to "examine how they were assessing their students."

Oliver had taught mathematics for seventeen years and thought he was pretty good. He'd developed entertaining demonstrations of some mathematical concepts and theorems, and had an easygoing lecture style that created a comfortable atmosphere in the classroom. Students knew he was always available after school for them. Over the past few years, though, he'd noticed that more students seemed to be trying hard but were really struggling, or were tuning out. Their fundamental understanding of mathematics seemed weaker every year. He wanted to do more for them, if he could. So when Oliver saw Bill's memo, he took it seriously. He spent some of his off-track time in July and August reading about alternative assessment and its impact on curriculum and instruction.

It was really because of his conversations with Lucy Dobbs, though, that he had launched his experiment in curriculum and assessment this September. Oliver smiled as he remembered his conversations with her. Thinking about Lucy always made him smile.

From the first day she joined the faculty of Grove High School a year earlier, Oliver had been impressed by Lucy's enthusiasm and energy, her creativity, and her knowledge of cutting-edge mathematics and education research. She quickly acquired a reputation among students as a great teacher. She and Oliver struck up a friendship. Often they ate lunch together, talking about mathematics, about their work, and about the particular joys and frustrations of teaching.

One day in September, Oliver and Lucy started talking about Bill's memo and Oliver's readings about alternative assessment. "I know that it's important to assess our kids differently," Oliver said, "and it's all tied up with teaching them differently, but I'm not sure I'm up to it. The logistics of giving them open-ended problems, having them work together, making them write about their thinking—that's all pretty new to me. I used to stand at the board and demonstrate a proof, and I'd look out and see maybe five confused faces. Now, I seem to see *twenty-five* confused faces. I want to reach those kids, but I don't really know if I can change the way I teach after all this time. Old dogs, you know. . . . "

Lucy laughed and said she thought he probably had a few tricks left in him. She also sympathized with him, remembering her own beginning attempts to craft mathematics lessons built on the students' own experiences and prior knowledge. "It wasn't a picnic! Half the time I felt completely lost, and I couldn't see or plan beyond how I was going to get through the day. But I started noticing that kids were getting drawn into the math in a way they hadn't been before. I realized how valuable their own ideas—even their mistakes—were in learning mathematics well, and how much more interested they seemed to be in working at it."

Lucy described one unit on geometry and architecture that had really excited the students. It had taught them a lot not only about geometry and architecture but also about how to ask their own questions and create multiple solutions to problems.

Oliver asked whether he might try it with his students.

"Of course you can!" Lucy found her lesson plans and gave them to him. "If you can't read my chicken scratches, or you just want to talk over some ideas, you know I'd love to help."

In early October, Oliver started the unit with his geometry students. He soon realized that active investigation, working and talking with classmates, writing, and thinking creatively about mathematics were as new and uncomfortable for them as they were for him. Still, he saw new glimmers of excitement and engagement in the students. The assessment that he conducted at the end of the month—the one on which Leti had gotten a C—showed that both he and the students had a good deal to learn about this new way of doing mathematics. While Oliver found it even more challenging than he had expected, he was encouraged by signs that he was reaching more of his students. They seemed more animated in class, and they were talking to one another more about mathematics and less about dates and video games. He had been pleasantly surprised several times by students' unexpected and insightful questions or unconventional solutions to problems. They were showing more interest and persistence, and more imagination in their work.

What Next?

Oliver's feelings of encouragement had now evaporated in the face of Mrs. Ramirez's questions and his own. He thought it would be really helpful to talk with Lucy, but she had recently gone off-track and was out of town. Oliver then decided to talk with Bill and get his perspective and guidance on what the math teachers should be doing to "think about the new ideas in assessment" and to "examine how they were assessing their students," as Bill had suggested in his memo. The day after Mrs. Ramirez's visit, he dropped by Bill's classroom.

"I didn't realize how many issues would start coming up when I tried to change something," he explained to Bill. "I thought I was just trying to get the kids more actively involved in the math, but now I'm worried about how to grade them, how to make cooperative groups really work, whether I even know how to teach them to communicate mathematically and think creatively, whether I'm doing them a disservice by not testing them in the usual way. I haven't felt this unsure since I was a first-year teacher."

Bill shook his head. "This is something you're going to have to figure out for yourself, Oliver. I can't tell you what to do. If you believe in the *Standards* and in alternative assessment, then you're going to have to make the changes. It's not a bad idea, with the CLAS tests coming. But you're going to have to figure out the way that's best for you. Personally, I think going slowly is the key—doing one thing at a time. That way you can be really sure of what you're doing."

Oliver walked out of Bill's office lost in thought and torn between two desires. He wanted to back off, and he wanted to forge ahead. He wanted to act with Bill's conservatism and caution, but would changing his practice "one thing at a time" make enough of a difference for his students? He wanted to have Lucy's boldness, but was it right to try something he wasn't sure about or comfortable with? He hadn't forgotten why he had tried something different in the first place: He wanted to help *all* his students understand and appreciate mathematics. But he just didn't know anymore what to do next.

Study Questions

1. What is this a case of?
2. What should Oliver do next? Why?
3. What support does Oliver have in his attempt to change his practice? What additional support, if any, does he need?

FACILITATOR'S GUIDE

Nancy Cali, Barbara Miller, Ilene Kantrov, and Cynthia Lang

Synopsis of Case

Oliver Wright, a mathematics teacher at Grove High School in Los Angeles, feels he isn't reaching many of his students and turns to an innovative colleague, Lucy Dobbs, for help. Oliver eventually decides to try teaching one of Lucy's units on geometry and architecture.

After assessing his students using a test that, like the unit itself, requires them to work together, find multiple solutions to problems, and communicate mathematically, Oliver is confronted by a concerned parent who fears that her child's tests will adversely affect her child's grades, ability to do well on standardized tests, and ability to get into college.

Oliver, disturbed by his meeting with the parent, realizes that he feels many uncertainties himself about the changes in curriculum and assessment that he has attempted. After talking with his department head, he isn't sure whether to revert to his usual teaching practice or to continue trying new things.

Major Issues

The purpose of this case is to promote discussion about issues that arise when an individual teacher decides to make significant changes in teaching practice. The case is designed to engage participants in thinking about various dimensions of change, including

- Reasons for attempting change, both personal incentives and external motivations
- Supports for and barriers to change
- Pace and scope of change
- Images of successful change

Guiding the Discussion

Discussion of this case and of the issues it raises can proceed in different ways, depending on the needs and experiences of the discussion participants. The five sets of questions offered here provide several ways to structure a conversation around issues of educational change. The questions are not meant to be a script for the facilitator and are certainly not exhaustive; they are intended only to suggest *some* of the questions and issues that might be fruitfully pursued.

1. Describing the Situation helps participants to articulate their perceptions of the problem described in the case and to uncover differences and similarities in their perspectives.
2. Exploring Contributing Factors asks participants to consider the many factors, internal and external to the main characters, that shape this particular case.
3. Articulating Possible Next Steps gives participants the opportunity to generate and analyze possible actions that the central characters could take.
4. Replaying the Case invites participants to think creatively about the case and to suggest different actions the characters could have taken that might have caused the case to evolve differently (and for the better).
5. Looking at the Bigger Picture helps participants consider the broad issues of change involved, using the case as a springboard for discussion.

Several different discussions can be structured with these sets of questions. A few possibilities:

- A discussion that moves from consideration of the specific details of Oliver's situation to consideration of broader and more general issues of individual change would use questions from all five sections.
- A discussion that concentrates mostly on the larger issues of change would use the case as a springboard, moving quickly through sections 1 and 2 and spending most of the time on section 5.

- A discussion that focuses on Oliver as a "test case" would move quickly through sections 1 and 2, spend more time on section 5, and then return to sections 3 and 4 to apply the ideas discussed.

- A discussion that considers the case's major themes throughout would raise questions from section 5 as participants move through sections 1, 2, 3, and 4.

The study questions at the end of the case appear again in the following sections and can be used as a focus for individual reflection in preparation for the discussion.

1. Describing the Situation

What is the problem in this case? Whose problem is it?

How would each of the characters in this case describe the problem? How is it similar and different for each of them?

What feelings do you think the problem has raised for each of the characters?

2. Exploring Contributing Factors.

What do you see as the factors influencing Oliver and his actions in this case? Factors might include

- The students' needs
- Oliver's growing awareness of the limits of his teaching approach
- Goals of the mathematics reform movement, as expressed in the NCTM *Standards*, the *California Mathematics Framework*, and so on.
- Oliver's relationship with Lucy and knowledge of her teaching practices
- Bill's memo regarding assessment strategies
- Oliver's knowledge of the eventual implementation of CLAS tests

What are some factors influencing the other participants' behavior and attitudes in this situation? Factors might include

- Parents' awareness and understanding of mathematics reform
- Students' and parents' expectations about grades and assessment
- Bill's meetings with other department heads about assessment
- Lucy's own experience with classroom change

What are other factors, not discussed in this case, that may have influenced the situation and Oliver's experiment? Some possible factors:

- Professional development opportunities (or the lack thereof) for Oliver and his colleagues
- Students' understanding (or lack thereof) of what Oliver was trying to do
- Encouragement (or lack thereof) from administrators for teachers' experimentation with new teaching methods and content
- Assessment practices beyond the school (e.g., college entrance exams)
- Mandates from the school district or the state concerning curriculum, instruction, scope and sequence, etc.

3. Articulating Possible Next Steps. What could Oliver do next? Some possible next steps:

- Oliver could back off completely and return to his former methods of teaching and assessment, which are more comfortable and predictable for him.
- Oliver could talk to Lucy, explain his situation and feelings, and ask her for advice.
- Oliver could ask for Mrs. Ramirez's help in forging a partnership with parents to explore and implement changes in mathematics curriculum and instruction.

What implications might each possible next step have for Oliver and his students? How might it improve or worsen the situation?

4. Replaying the Case. What might Oliver have done differently at any point in the story? How might it have changed the evolution or outcome of the case? Some possible ideas:

- Oliver might have gone to Bill before actually initiating the changes to ask for suggestions and help in how to proceed; Bill might have been more supportive later.
- Oliver might have focused in the geometry and architecture unit on only one new aspect, for instance, students' problem-solving skills, and emphasized these skills on the test; the assessment might have produced better results.
- Oliver might have arranged for Lucy or another colleague to observe his classes and give him feedback along the way, before the assessment; he might have anticipated problems and adjusted his teaching accordingly.

What supports or impediments might Oliver have encountered in each different scenario? What might other characters have done differently that would have changed the outcome of Oliver's experiment?

5. Looking at the Bigger Picture

Reasons for change. Oliver was motivated to try something new because of his own perceptions of his students' needs, Lucy's innovative teaching practices, and Bill's memo asking him to think about new ideas in assessment.

Was each of these influences beneficial to Oliver? harmful? neutral?

How does it matter if the impetus to change is internal? external? Does the impetus for change affect a teacher's perspective on change in general?

What, if any, factors are necessary to promote change by an individual teacher?

Support for and barriers to change. Oliver looked to both Lucy and Bill for support in changing his practice, with different results.

What was the nature of the support for Oliver's changing his teaching? Was it sufficient? What were the barriers that Oliver faced? Were they prohibitive?

What kinds of support are needed for educators to change their practice? Are there any conditions or supports that are *usually* necessary for change to be successful? How can they ensure that the needed supports are there?

What are the typical barriers to change that educators face? Are there any barriers that *usually* doom change attempts? How can those who attempt change circumvent or overcome barriers to change?

To what extent is an individual's past experience with change a support or a barrier to current efforts to effect change?

Is it possible for an individual to change successfully without others also changing? Does an individual have to enlist the support or understanding of others (colleagues, administrators, parents, students) in order to make change successful?

Pace and scope of change. By trying one of Lucy's innovative units, Oliver tried to teach and assess mathematics in ways that were new for him and for his students.

Would Oliver have felt differently about his efforts if he had altered the scope or pace of his changes?

Which changes are best done slowly? quickly? On what does the answer depend?

When is it best to attempt comprehensive changes? smaller or partial changes?

Images of successful change. While he was encouraged by what he was seeing among his students, Oliver's conversation with Mrs. Ramirez caused him to doubt his efforts.

How do you think Oliver would assess his efforts at change so far? How would you assess them?

In what ways are mistakes, false starts, or failures a part of change? How many setbacks are acceptable?

What are short-term markers of success that individuals need to identify when attempting change? How can teachers and others gauge the overall or long-term success of a change effort, in the midst of problems or uncertainties? Should they rely only on their own judgment?

In what ways are successful changes finished products? In what ways are they ongoing processes?

SUGGESTED READING

Barnett, C., D. Goldenstein, and B. Jackson. 1994. *Fractions, Decimals, Ratios, and Percents: Hard to Teach and Hard to Learn* and *Facilitator's Discussion Guide*. Portsmouth, NH: Heinemann.

EDC/EES (Education Development Center and Educational Extension Service of The Michigan Partnership for New Education). 1995. *Faces of Equity* (video cases and print materials, including *Facilitator's Guide*.) East Lansing, MI: Michigan State University Board of Trustees and The Michigan Partnership for New Education.

Kleinfeld, J. ed. 1989. *Teaching Cases in Cross-Cultural Education*. Fairbanks: University of Alaska.

Kleinfeld, J., and S. Yerian, eds. 1995. *Gender Tales: Tensions in the Schools*. New York: St. Martin's Press.

Merseth, K., and J. Karp. Harvard Project on Schooling and Children. 1997. Harvard Mathematics Case Development Project 1994–1997. (Harvard Project on Schooling and Children Working Paper. Cambridge, MA.) For ordering information, please call (617)496-6883 or email hpsc@harvard.edu.

Mesa-Bains, A., and J. Shulman. 1994. *Diversity in the Classroom: A Casebook for Teachers and Teacher Educators, Facilitator's Guide*. Hillsdale, NJ: Research for Better Schools and Lawrence Erlbaum Associates.

Miller, B., and I. Kantrov, eds. 1998. *Casebook on School Reform*. Portsmouth, NH: Heinemann.

Schifter, D., ed. 1996. *What's Happening in Math Class? Vol. 1: Envisioning New Practices Through Teacher Narratives*. New York: Teachers College Press.

———1996. *What's Happening in Math Class? Vol. 2: Reconstructing Professional Identities*. New York: Teachers College Press.

Shulman, J., and A. Mesa-Bains, eds. 1993. *Diversity in the Classroom: A Casebook for Teachers and Teacher Educators*. Hillsdale, NJ: Research for Better Schools and Lawrence Erlbaum Associates.

Silverman, R., W. Welty, and S. Lyon. 1992. *Case Studies for Teacher Problem Solving*. New York: McGraw-Hill.

Wassermann, S. 1993. *Getting Down to Cases: Learning to Teach with Case Studies*. New York: Teachers College Press.

Yerian, S. 1995. *Gender Tales: Tensions in the Schools, Instructor's Manual*. New York: St. Martin's Press.

BIBLIOGRAPHY

Ames, N., and E. Miller. 1994. *Changing Middle Schools: How to Make Schools Work for Young Adolescents*. San Francisco: Jossey-Bass.

Barnett, C., and S. Sather. 1992. "Using Case Discussions to Promote Changes in Beliefs Among Mathematics Teachers." Unpublished manuscript presented at American Educational Research Association Annual Meeting, San Francisco.

Brubaker, D., and L. Simon. 1993. *Teachers as Decision Makers: Real-Life Cases to Hone Your People Skills*. Newbury Park, CA: Corwin.

Doyle, W. 1990. "Case Methods in Teacher Education." *Teacher Education Quarterly* 17 (1): 7–15.

EDC/EES (Education Development Center and Educational Extension Service of The Michigan Partnership for New Education). 1995. *Faces of Equity*. East Lansing, MI: Michigan State University Board of Trustees and The Michigan Partnership for New Education.

Kagan, D. 1993. "Contexts for the Use of Classroom Cases." *American Educational Research Journal* 30 (4): 703–723.

Kleinfeld, J. 1990. "The Special Virtues of the Case Method in Preparing Teachers for Minority Schools." *Teacher Education Quarterly* 17 (1): 43–52.

———. 1992. "Learning to Think Like a Teacher." In *Case Methods in Teacher Education*, ed. J. Shulman, 33–49. New York: Teachers College Press.

Merseth, K. 1991. *The Case for Cases*. Washington, DC: American Association for Higher Education.

———. 1992. "Cases for Decision Making in Teacher Education." In *Case Methods in Teacher Education*, ed. J. Shulman, 50–63. New York: Teachers College Press.

Miller, B., I. Kantrov, and J. Hunault. 1996. "Windows and Mirrors: Designing Video Cases to Promote Teacher Inquiry." Presented as part of a symposium, "Designing Innovative Video for Teachers' Professional Development." American Educational Research Association Annual Meeting, New York.

Richert, A. 1992. "Writing Cases: A Vehicle for Inquiry into the Teaching Process." In *Case Methods in Teacher Education*, ed. J. Shulman, 155–174. New York: Teachers College Press.

Schifter, D., ed. 1996. *What's Happening in Math Class? Vol. 2: Reconstructing Professional Identities*. New York: Teachers College Press.

Shulman, J. 1990. "Now You See Them, Now You Don't: Anonymity Versus Visibility in Case Studies of Teachers." *Educational Researcher* 19 (6): 11–15.

———. 1992. "Teacher-Written Cases with Commentaries: A Teacher-Researcher Collaboration. In *Case Methods in Teacher Education*, ed. J. Shulman, 131–152. New York: Teachers College Press.

Shulman, L. 1987. "Knowledge and Teaching: Foundations of the New Reform." *Harvard Educational Review* 57 (1): 1–22.

———. 1990. "Reconnecting Foundations to the Substance of Teacher Education." *Teachers College Record* 91 (3): 300–310.

———. 1992. "Toward a Pedagogy of Cases." In *Case Methods in Teacher Education*, ed. J. Shulman, 1–30. New York: Teachers College Press.

Sykes, G., and T. Bird. 1992. "Teacher Education and the Case Idea." *Review of Research in Education* 18: 457–521.

Wassermann, S. 1993. *Getting Down to Cases: Learning to Teach with Case Studies*. New York: Teachers College Press.